ACTOR'S CHOICE:
Monologues for Teens

ACTOR'S CHOICE:

Monologues for Teens

Edited by Erin Detrick

New York, NY

Actor's Choice: Monologues for Teens is published by Playscripts, Inc., 325 West 38th Street, Suite 305, New York, New York, 10018, www.playscripts.com

Cover design by Another Limited Rebellion
Text design and layout by Jason Pizzarello

First Edition: April 2008
10 9 8 7 6 5 4 3 2 1

Editor's Note: In some of the monologues in this book, dialogue or stage directions from the play may have been removed for clarity's sake.

Library of Congress Cataloging-in-Publication Data

Actor's choice : monologues for teens / edited by Erin Detrick.
    p. cm.
  Summary: "Collection of monologues from the Playscripts, Inc. catalog of plays, representing a variety of American playwrights. The source material for each monologue may be found on the Playscripts website, where nearly the entire text of every play can be read for free. Intended for teenage actors"--Provided by publisher.
  ISBN-13: 978-0-9709046-6-9 (pbk.)
  1. Monologues. 2. Acting. 3. American drama--20th century. 4. Teenagers--Drama. I. Detrick, Erin, 1981-
  PN2080.A287 2008
  808.82'45--dc22
                    2007050166

Acknowledgments

First and foremost, this book was made possible by all of the exceptionally talented playwrights who so generously allowed us to include their work. We are deeply appreciative.

Special thanks are due to Jason Pizzarello, Doug Briggs, and Devin McKnight for their monumental contributions to the creation of this book. Thanks also to Noah Scalin, Terry Nemeth, and Arthur Stanley.

Table of Contents

Female 51

Male or Female

INTRODUCTION

Finding the perfect monologue can be a complicated task. You need a strong, juicy piece of material that will highlight your talents—preferably a piece that hasn't been seen thousands of times already. Furthermore, to fully understand the context of your monologue, you need the play itself at your fingertips to help you prepare. Often that play is impossible to track down. That's where *Actor's Choice* comes in.

We at Playscripts, Inc. have long looked forward to creating a book of monologues drawn from the 1000+ plays we publish. There's a wealth of engaging, dynamic monologues found within those plays—and we're thrilled to make many of them available to you now.

But here's what makes *Actor's Choice* truly unique: For every monologue, you have the option of reading up to 90% of the play it comes from, all from one source, and all for free. Simply visit the Playscripts, Inc. website at *www.playscripts.com*. No longer do you have to waste time searching for a script— the work's already done for you.

On behalf of all the exceptional playwrights represented in this book, we hope that you enjoy these monologues, and that you get the part!

HOW TO USE THIS BOOK

Every monologue in this book is preceded by a brief description that introduces the context. If you'd like to read the play itself, we've made the process simple:

o   Go to the Playscripts, Inc. website: **www.playscripts.com**

o   Run a search for the play title.

o   Click the *Read Sample* link and read away.

o   If you'd like to read the entire play, you may order a book at any time from the Playscripts, Inc. website.

FOREWORD

Confessions of a Broadway Casting Director

I was a year out of college when I went on my first audition in New York City. A friend of mine had left school after getting cast in a national tour, and when one of his fellow actors dropped out, he got me an audition to replace her. I was living in Virginia at the time, so I quickly planned a trip to the big city. I still remember driving over the Verrazano Bridge, nervous with anticipation, and heading to my friend's apartment in Queens. I had picked an outfit, rested my voice, and agonized over which song I should sing. The next day at the audition I walked into the room and sang my song, following all the audition rules I'd learned in college. When I finished I turned expectantly to the casting director. She looked down at my headshot, and then back at me with a slightly confused look and said, "So, who do you—where did…you…come from?" When I explained that my friend was in the tour, it was as if a light went on in her head. She nodded knowingly; my appearance in the casting call suddenly made sense. Even with my lack of big city audition experience, I knew this was not a good sign. I had clearly made some rookie mistakes, I didn't get the part, and I left New York feeling I had blown my big chance.

I moved to New York City shortly thereafter and only lasted a year before I gave up acting. Fortunately, I found another great vocation—on the other side of the table as a casting director. If I knew then what I know now, that first audition would have gone a lot differently.

I truly believe that actors have one of the hardest jobs around. Just look at the audition situation alone—actors have to be charming but not arrogant, vulnerable but not needy, friendly but not so friendly that the people on the other side of the table start to get scared. They have to be interesting, brilliant, moving, memorable, and right for the part. Often all in three minutes or less.

Some audition tips are obvious. Then again, I've still seen each of the following scenarios on several occasions, so perhaps these tips bear repeating…

o Don't stand too close to the person behind the table. Firstly because it's an invasion of personal space, and secondly because a little distance helps us with perspective.

o If there is a reader present for your audition, please don't excessively touch or molest them. Unfortunately, I've seen it happen often and it's uncomfortable for everyone.

o If your audition involves reading a scene, don't worry about memorizing lines unless you've been asked to. I'd much rather watch an actor refer to pages and be in the moment, than watch them mentally panic over what the next line is.

o Always second-guess the use of props, and the amount of the audition you spend lying on, crawling across, rolling around on, or throwing yourself to the floor. You don't have to tell me which special skills on your resume make you really right for this and how much you want this part. I know you want this part, as I assume you wouldn't be here if you didn't.

o And finally, unless we know each other, it's probably best to leave your personal life out of the audition room. I've had people tell me about everything from brain tumors to painful divorces. And while I'd happily hear about your life over a cup of coffee, the audition room is not the right forum for it.

What many actors don't know is that the people on the other side of the table are actually on your side. We desperately want you to be our answer. We want you to be brilliant just as badly as you want to be brilliant. The best auditions I've seen have been when actors come in the room simply as themselves. Don't waste your energy trying to figure out who or what you think we want you to be. Be who you are. It's always more interesting. Because as much as this is going to sound like your mother talking, there is no one out there like you. No one brings exactly the same things to a scene or monologue that you do. So find out what it is that you are able to relate to in a character and explore it. And when you do, figure out where the vulnerability is. In every audition, you've got to create a compelling character. Finding the vulnerability means that I get to see exactly what that character is really feeling, even if it's ugly or embarrassing. And that is always fascinating to watch.

The monologues in this book do half of the work for you. They are fresh, truthful, and interesting, not to mention brand-new material (which means I won't be comparing you to the girl/guy who used your same monologue five people ago). If you can deliver a monologue that is genuine, natural, and has vulnerability to it, even if you're not right for whatever I might be casting that day, I will put you in my "Remember Them" file and keep you in mind for other opportunities down the road. In the long run, so much of casting has to do with tiny details that are beyond your control. So do yourself a favor. Show up, give a truthful performance, and let the rest go. You are enough.

Again, if only I had known that, who knows how my first audition in New York would have turned out...!

Kate Schwabe
Associate Casting Director, Jim Carnahan Casting
Roundabout Theatre Company, New York City

Male

THE 1ST ANNUAL ACHADAMEE AWARDS
(full-length version)

Alan Haehnel

Norman receives a nomination for the best male actor (liar) at Achadamee High School. This monologue shows him at work.

NORMAN. I ain't afraid of you, man. No way I'm afraid of you. You want to fight me? I'll fight you. Don't you even think I won't fight you, man. Bring it on—any time! Right now? Uh, now's not actually a good time for me. A chicken? Me? You calling me a chicken? Is that what you're saying? Oh, man, you're not going to get away with that. Nobody calls me a chicken. Nobody. It don't matter to me that you're taller by five inches or that you outweigh me by a hundred pounds. Don't even think it bothers me that you're three times Golden Glove champion and that you've been invited as a guest commentator for the Ultimate Fighting League. So what? That's nothing! If you get me mad—and let me tell you, you're getting close!—then you just better watch out! I don't care if you're Superman. Or the Amazing Hulk. Or any of those 'cause I'll take you on just the same. I ain't afraid of you; I ain't afraid of nobody! Nobody! You hearing me? So you just better back off. Right now! Just back away and you won't have to get trounced! I'm telling you, you take one more step and I will not be held responsible for what I do! *(He watches, as if his adversary has stepped closer. He looks up.)* Oh, yeah? I ain't afraid of you, and if my mother didn't need me home right now, you'd be dead meat.

(He runs away.)

THE 1ST ANNUAL ACHADAMEE AWARDS
(full-length version)

Alan Haehnel

Nigel receives a nomination for the best male actor (liar) at Achadamee High School. This monologue shows him at work.

NIGEL. Before I begin my oral presentation on the play *Hamlet*, I would like to take just a moment to clear the air about a few things. I understand that some nasty rumors have been going around about me. Rumor one: I have never even read the play *Hamlet*. The book has been in the bottom of my locker, unopened since the first day we got the assignment. Rumor two: I don't know a thing about *Hamlet*. Up until yesterday morning, I thought a *Hamlet* was a clever name for a small breakfast item. According to that rumor, I even went to Denny's and tried to order a Hamlet with a side of home fries. Rumor three: I am completely unprepared for this presentation, and all I plan to do is get a barely passing grade by standing up here and bluffing my way through until my time is up. And rumor four, the most sickening one of all: I, Nigel Thorburn, have no academic motivation whatsoever. I expend the least amount of energy possible to squeak by, using only my natural charm and extreme talents in the art of slinging the bull. I want to say, right here and right now, that I highly resent these rumors. If any of you have been spreading them, I say—pardon my language, please—damn you. Damn your conniving hearts and your lying mouths. To those of you who have begun to doubt me because of these rumors, I say listen! For I am about to deliver a presentation on *Hamlet* that will erase all doubt, all fear, all worry, all…excuse me? What? My time is up? Do you mean to say I'll be getting a D- for simply using up my time even though I haven't yet begun to reveal the great mysteries of the play *Hamlet*? I will? I am appalled. But, I accept my fate without complaint. Hey, that almost rhymed. I am good!

AND A CHILD SHALL LEAD

Michael Slade

Terezin Concentration Camp, 1942. Martin Lowy, 10, separated from his family, tries to hold onto some sense of normalcy by documenting his life in the camp in letters to his brother. The letters can never be mailed, and if caught writing them, Martin can be killed.

MARTIN. *(Writing a letter.)*

Dear Brother,

It may seem strange that I am writing you, since I don't know where you are, and couldn't mail this letter even if I did. But I will write you anyway and save the letters until we see each other again. I am in Terezin. Barrack L-318. It is about sixty kilometers from Prague, and it used to be a fort. But not anymore. There are many grown-ups, and many children. The older kids have to work in underground factories during the day. But we have a secret school where we study and write and draw pictures. I like drawing the best. We aren't given paper. But yesterday around dusk, I saw a soldier throwing out some forms. I hid for a long time until I was sure he was gone. It was very scary. Then I snuck over to the trash barrel, reached in, grabbed the forms, shoved them in my shirt, and made it back to the barracks. The forms have German writing all over them. I don't know what it says. But the backs are blank. I wish I was home in Prague with you and Mommy and Daddy. I don't like it here. The other kids make fun of me. But at least I can draw. I drew a picture of our home, so I'll remember it. And I'm drawing a picture of me in Terezin for you, so you'll remember me. See you soon. Love, Martin.

The Birds: A Modern Adaptation

Don Zolidis

Eulpides has fled the world of mankind and joined the kingdom of the birds. Here he recounts his harrowing and hilarious childhood as an outcast.

EULPIDES. I can't wait to be a bird. This may surprise you, but I've always thought I was a little bit of a disaster as a human being. I mean, after my Mom abandoned me and all, and before I started stalking girls who hated me, I was an unpopular child. Little old ladies who passed me on the street would try to toss me in front of moving cars. They'd scream something about doing society a favor and then whoop, there I'd be, right in the middle of traffic, the drivers swerving every which way to avoid denting their hoods on my prone little body. That's mostly what I remember from childhood. That and the hordes of angry rats which used to chase me down alleys. Maybe my luck's gonna change. What do you think?

THE BROTHERS GRIMM SPECTACULATHON
(full-length version)

Don Zolidis

After learning that his daughter is being pressured into kissing a frog, a nostalgic King tries to explain why it's important to go out there and embrace amphibians, or geeks.

KING. Let me tell you a little story about your father when he was your age: You see, I was something of a dork.

I was. I was. I played Dungeons and Dragons. I read comic books. I wasn't very good at sports. I spent a lot of time on-line. I had unfortunate clothes. And there was a girl who I was friends with. And she was beautiful. Absolutely gorgeous. And we used to walk home from school every day and she'd tell me all the problems she was having with whatever popular boy she was dating at the time, and I'd listen, and I'd listen, and I listened to her every day. And she would always say, "why can't they be nice like you?" I was in love with that girl. And I just kept waiting for my chance. Until one day she had gotten dumped by her latest jerk and she came over to my house in the middle of the night after getting drunk at a party, and it was raining outside and she gave me this huge hug. I thought, now's my chance. So I leaned in to kiss her—

And she said, "what are you doing? I don't want to ruin our friendship." It was as if my heart had been ripped from my chest and popped like a grape. And she looked down at the crushed, oozing juice of my soul and said, "um...I don't think so." Like she had dismembered my love with a meat cleaver and used the blood-spattered wreckage of my life as a cage liner for her pet cockatiel Ramon to poop on. As if she—

Well after I became King girls started to like me. Go figure. But what I'm telling you is this: Get back in that room and kiss that damn frog! Kiss him for all the losers and the dorks out there who never got kissed by their princesses! Kiss him for that guy in the audience who thinks he's on a date but really isn't because she doesn't like him like that! Kiss him for that guy who came here thinking he was going to meet chicks and found out that every girl in here was already taken by some jerk! Kiss him for the sad, the weird, the skinny, the not-all-that-athletic and the guys with the pungent body odor problems who should probably shower more frequently! KISS THE DAMN FROG!

THE CANTERVILLE GHOST

adapted by Marisha Chamberlain
from the story by Oscar Wilde

In an ancient manor house in rural Cheshire, England, circa 1910, the ghost who has long haunted the place and inspired fear far and wide, now finds himself beset with new owners of the house—skeptical Americans.

GHOST. I have been having a little rest in my coffin and thinking a little thought. These Americans really need to be taught a lesson. They're simply begging for it. And I am sure I can satisfy. It is a grand plan, thoroughly orchestrated: I begin at midnight, of course, in the master bedchamber where I plan to seize the professor by the ankles, gibber at him from the foot of the bed and stab myself three times in the throat to the sound of slow music.

(Raises dagger.)

What do you think of this? Oh, I already showed you this, didn't I? Could I be losing my concentration? Hardly seems possible. In ghost circles, my concentration has been absolutely unrivalled for three hundred years. Bother it! Back to the task at hand:

(Stabs himself three times in the throat. Giggles.)

All right then. Having reduced Professor Otis to a trembling jelly, I shall place a clammy hand on Mrs. Otis's forehead, while I hiss into the professor's ear the awful details of the day when she shall die!

(Pauses for effect. Sheaths the dagger.)

On to the daughter's room. Now, the daughter has never insulted me in any way and she is rather pretty and gentle and so on, but to be thorough I shall have to deal her a hollow groan or two from the wardrobe and if time permits, grabble at the counterpane with palsy twitching fingers. *(Demonstrates.)*

And finally, on to the boys, oh, they shall be my chief pleasure, the little insects! First, I shall hover over their beds and place a heavy foot on each of their chests, producing the stifling sensation of nightmare… Did I mention grabbling at the counterpane in the daughter's room? Grabble at the counterpane with palsy twitching fingers? I did, didn't I. Where am I? What am I doing? Oh, yes: I am stifling the boys. Then, *then*, standing between their beds in the form of a green, icy cold corpse, til they come fully awake and paralyzed with fear, I shall as my final sensation, throw off my winding sheet and crawl round the room with bleached white bones and one rolling eyeball in the character of "Dumb Daniel, or the Suicide's Skeleton." Any questions?

Chicken Bones for the Teenage Soup

Alan Haehnel

Kevin delivers his "inspirational" graduation speech that urges graduates to simply accept their lot in life. Striving for anything more is futile.

KEVIN. *(In cap and gown, as if delivering a graduation speech:)* Members of the school board, Principal Clark, Superintendent Morrison, parents and relatives, and, of course, members of the class of 2004: As your class president for the past four years, I have had the privilege of leading and advising you on many occasions. I am grateful for this last opportunity before we depart to pursue our separate paths. And on this day of commencement, I would like you all to ponder one crucial word: Acceptance.

Who knows how many times and in how many places across this nation of ours this famous cliché will be spoken: Today is the first day of the rest of your life. I don't disagree with this quote at all. Obviously, it is true. However, I need you to understand the dangerous assumption hiding beneath this statement. The assumption is that, if today is the first day of the rest of your life, then the days that are to come hold the promise of something better than we have experienced so far. This, however, is not true. And that brings me back to the concept of acceptance.

My fellow graduates, I urge you to accept the fact that most of the goals you have for your life will not be met. Some of you are dreaming of becoming movie stars, professional athletes, great writers, wealthy lawyers, or high-ranking public officials. Given the social climate and families from which you come, though, these goals are completely unrealistic. Give it up.

Some will tell you that the key to success lies in fostering strong relationships with others. But you, my classmates, should accept the fact that your particular circle of friends and relations will do nothing to help you reach success. Holding on to these relationships will simply help you perpetuate your present, pitiful situation. But that is all right. You are who you are and, since birds of a feather flock together, you are not going to change anything substantially in terms of your relationships. In short, hold on to the friends you have because even lousy, inconsequential friends are better than no friends at all.

Finally, graduates, accept the fact that the habits you have now are the habits you will continue to have for the rest of your life. They, along with heredity and social conditioning, pretty much entirely control you. Accept the fact that your attempts to better yourself will be met with so much resistance, both internally and externally, that the effort is essentially wasted. Accept the fact that you are a slob and you are destined to become exactly like the slobs who raised you.

The sooner you can learn to accept these truths, my fellow graduates, the sooner you will be able to settle in to an unchallenging but not-too-bad life full of adequate food, bad television, and one or two major addictions. In conclusion, let me end with another amended cliché: Be all you can be. Just accept that all you can be just ain't all that much.

Thank-you.

COUNTING TO INFINITY

Max Posner

A young man stuck in limbo between his familiar childhood landscape and a mysterious future describes his appointment with a doctor who has assessed his progress in becoming a grown man.

BOY. Seventy one, seventy two, seventy three. He asks me to drop my pants as politely as possible. I do, awkwardly. He's looking at me and I just look straight ahead. The silence is deadly. This man is peering through a window, my window into the deepest, deepest something. He asks me to cough and is looking at me. The silence is so deadly. The kind of silence that says more than words ever will. It's funny. I let out a little laugh. I have to do something. I have to make the awkward silence all the more awkward. After I laugh, he feels inclined to say "it's a bit ticklish down there, huh?" And I of course have no choice but to nod, but I hadn't been laughing because it was ticklish. He says I'm progressing. Slowly. He takes off his rubber gloves and I put on my pants, as quickly as possible. For a moment he looks at me. He looks me in the eye. Not as a child for once. He looks me in the eye as if I were an adult. I'd been wishing he would, but now that he is I don't know if I like it. I don't know if I want to be like him.

THE DEATH OF KING ARTHUR

Matthew Freeman

A Page Boy dreams of adventures and meeting his hero, King Arthur.

PAGE. Today my trusty blade lays lonesome siege to the strong-hold of a Beast. Why lonesome? The blade, my wooden rapier, is alone today, but does a valiant hero need more than strength and purity? Ah no! A man once told me that if I kept my intentions pure and course just, I would be rewarded. The only thing I questioned is the reward! Is honor and goodness not its own reward? By Arthur, I have learned that courage makes a Knight, and that might comes after right. I could be with him, one day, not too many years. When I am taller, and battle beasts, and travel to the Land of Gore, to save the Maid Melinda, a pretty girl, from the wiry blood-roots and the Black Sorcerer. My wooden rapier made sharper with use, you see, so that I know its weight and wield it skillful. The sweet Melinda leaps into my arms and as she loves my goodness and my dedication, is married to me before the King. But not before I've faced above a pit of fire, her captor and outwitten him with charms and riddles. He'd say: "Stand down, small knight! Your age impedes your might!" And I, with the Maiden's hand in mine, quip: "Mother says as much and told me that before, as early as this morning…long before I felled the Sorcerer and Roots! But you know as much as Mother, villain, there's none too young for bravery!" And by Excalibur, he'd pause for thinking of a retort, and in his leg! Then ARM! Then…other ARM! Then heart! I'd stick him with my blade. A married, holy, truthful hero. Can you see me then? I'm not noble, I know. But Arthur was raised by farmers, as was I. I'll see him, and he'll see me in him and likewise. And, I'll carry what I must, I'll teach them all a move or two with my cutter! Some will tell him No…like mother…but Kings know who is good. When I am older, just a few short months, I'll go to Camelot and serve the king. I will be the Child of the Round Table.

EMPLOYEES MUST WASH HANDS…
BEFORE MURDER

Don Zolidis

Torok is the weasely manager of a low-end fast food restaurant, the Burgtorium. His methods may require congressional oversight.

TOROK. Good. Now, in the Burgatorium team, we like to do things a certain way. Before you do something, ask yourself this question: Will someone sue me? If the answer to that question is no, then you go ahead and do it. If the answer to that question is yes, do it very quietly. And then sign your name to it. And then sign this form releasing the store of any responsibility.

> *(He produces a form.* TOROK *guides the new employee over to the counter area.)*

You got your counters here, this is where we talk to the customers, and then the customers eat their stuff over there and then run to the restrooms, which are located on either side of us— Behind the counter is the kitchen area, which is where the magic happens. You are gonna start out in the kitchen, and if you can handle it, you just might move up to the counter. The counter, though, requires a whole different skill set. Like pressing buttons. And talking. But most important: listening. Because if you look at the customers, they just might tell you what they want. And then you have to press buttons. And talk some more. It's complicated.

A lot of people go to school a long time to learn these skills. *(He stares at her.)* Perhaps this short instructional video will help you un-der-stand the history of the Bugatorium. I'm going to go play solitaire on my computer to pass the time and deaden my soul.

EVERYTHING SO FAR

C. Denby Swanson and Doug Rand

Dead Peter serves as narrator in a world of dinosaurs, lab monkeys, uprooted flowers, and other stories adapted from a textbook on biology. He winds up going backwards in time, from death to life, to experience his moment of most perfect peace.

DEAD PETER. Hi. I'm Peter.

I'm dead.

Don't worry. It happens.

Do you know my Uncle Abe? He's alive. You'll meet him tonight.

Do you know Betsy? Uncle Abe's dinosaur. For real. She's alive, too. Uncle Abe says that she's older than he is, but she seems young to me.

But I guess just because you're alive doesn't mean you know everyone. It's not like a small club.

Who else—let's see.

Some musicians.

A biologist.

A fly. He's only got 24 hours to live.

I feel close to him.

Some flowers.

A bunch of other people.

It's kind of cool being dead. Being alive was confusing for me. Being dead is so certain. It sounds funny. Dead Peter. I got here. It's final. That's that. Dead Peter.

I remember the first moment I realized that's what I was. I was walking to the subway platform and I fell suddenly, flat down on my face. But nothing—felt. It wasn't that I couldn't feel, like being in shock, or being—well. I don't know. Just being. It was that nothing felt. I wasn't *being* anymore. Right in the middle of a conversation. Right in the middle of talking up this beautiful girl on the subway platform. I almost got her phone number.

Dead Peter. That's what I realized I had become. But if you could look at me now, if you could unbury my body right now, you'd see that I'm all fungus now. Fungus Peter. Fungus Peter. Things living off me. So really, I live.

That's kind of weird, huh.

Other organisms make me into their house, they make me into their back yard. This is all figuratively speaking, you understand. A whole group of creatures sort of move in when you're dead. They are making me, my body, into their job, the grocery store, a good school for their kids.

It's neat. I don't know what else life is except those things. So I am still alive. My uncle Abe thinks I'm alive also, but in a different way, and it's confusing for his wife, Bathsheba. Did I mention Bathsheba? You'll meet her, too. Give them just a second. They'll be right out.

FEEDING ON MULBERRY LEAVES

Lucinda McDermott

17-year-old Jeb Stuart Flint desires to escape the confines of the Virginia mountains and spin his dream of becoming a fashion designer in the canyons of New York City. He offers up a prayer to who ever may be listening.

JEB. Hello? Anybody out there? Jeb here. Guess you know that being all knowing and powerful, right? I'm not sure about this God thing. I like the idea of a fairy godmother. Yeah. Or godfather— hey, I ain't prejudiced. I mean, it worked for Cinderella, right? Guess I'm lookin' for a little divine intervention here. See, my family runs this store near the Natural Bridge of Virginia. Guess you know that, too. Seventh Natural Wonder of the World, by God— or, whatever. Yeah, we buy squirrel tails and ginseng. Got black and gold ceramic plaques of The Last Supper. It's the Land 'o Little Debbies, cigarettes and gasoline. Something for everybody, right? Nah. What I need ain't here. Now, if you don't mind, this is where I'm hoping you'll come in. I need…magic, a miracle… I need… See, I got this dream. On a clear night, outside my bedroom window—you can see a huge slice of sky with a slight hump of Stoner's Mountain. The sky is a delicious cobalt blue, and I'm a Matisse cut-out. Running. Looking for others to hold hands with— to dance over hills shaped like the curves of a woman—to dance to the hum of the industrial revolution. Needle and thread marrying with cloth. The hum of coming together. All us separate, cocooned beings join in the dance. Over the hills, up the mountain. For once, no longer alone. We rise. We float. Up, up, into that night sky.

GOVERNING ALICE

C. Denby Swanson

Ethan is high school valedictorian and a young man with a secret. This would have been his graduation speech had he not been killed in the course of robbing a local convenience store.

ETHAN. Aristotle said, We are what we repeatedly do. Excellence, then, is not an act but a habit. We will arrange flowers, electrons, words and water. We'll shape politics, policies, the census, the economy, the atmosphere, the environment. We'll be productive and worthwhile. We will turn out to be Really Good People.

In reality, we are full of secrets. We have lives and interests and talents. Things we do. Those secret things. Most are independent of Latin and Trig, Honor Society, our jobs, sometimes our families. We have secrets that develop alongside our college applications, our team sports. What are the secrets of any given eighteen year old?

Maybe nothing I could say will make a difference. Maybe I'm just a liar. My good advice? What. Be true to yourself. Set goals. Work hard. Get fired. Steal for the first time. Like it. Shove the money in your book bag. Walk in a little late. Smile. Fool everyone. I could say anything, and you will wind up mesmerized. Or maybe you'll be inspired for a day. I've been stealing from you for years like that and you haven't noticed. You still don't notice. Go to the graduation parties. Pull out your hip flasks. Don't drink. Don't take stuff that isn't yours. Who says no? You will forget.

Hazard County

Allison Moore

Chad, a 17-year-old high school student, white. He is middle-class, wears slightly urban/hip-hop clothes. Speaks with a slight drawl, but nothing comic. He occasionally uses rap or hip-hop gestures. He explains why he bought a 1969 Charger and painted it to look like the "General Lee."

CHAD. People think it's cool, I guess. I mean, it's—you know, I'm out, and people know it's me, they know right away "Chad's pulling up," whatever, because, you know, not everybody has a General Lee. So it causes a stir, a little bit of a stir. I like that.

(Very exaggerated and slightly aggressive:)

"The Chicks Dig It."

(Laughs.)

Naw. I mean,

(As before:)

I mean THEY DO.

(Pause. Then smile.)

I've been working on it for about 4 years. My dad used to race stockcars. And we were out one day because he wanted to look at this '68 Cutlass Supreme? So we go around back a this guy's house to check out his set up, and there it is, '69 Charger up on blocks. Total POS, engine completely out, but I flipped, because it's the exact right year.

Some a my friends tried to make fun me at first, 'cause I was like building a car I couldn't even drive? But now they're like "Dawg, that car is rip!" And "Lemme drive it, catch some air, do it Duke-style" all that. My buddy Clay even got the Luke Duke Slide down, you know, where he slides across the hood and then jumps in the car?

We were out one time, on our way up to Clay's cabin, and we stop at this gas station. And this guy, total fucking hick, he sees the car and he starts in, just "Yeeeeee-haw!" All the way across the parking lot, just "Yee-haw!" like they did in the show. And Clay's all "Check this cracker." And the guy starts heading right for us, which I'm pretty used to now, and most folks are nice. But he's just this— got the gap teeth, and scraggly-ass hair, fucking reeks of, like, piss and Colt 45, and he's all "Lookie here! It's Bo and Luke! All the way from Hazzard County!" And we talk for a minute, and finally I'm like, I gotta go, nice to know ya. And I unlock the door and he flips. "You ain't even welded the doors shut! You can't have a General Lee with doors that open! Boy, you got to slide through the window."

And Clay looks at the guy and says, real serious: "I know it never rained in Hazzard, sir, but it sure does come down sometimes in Conyers." And the guy looks confused, he's like, "What?" And Clay says, "Well, Bo and Luke could weld their doors shut, but my friend here sure doesn't want his interior to get wet when it rains." And the guy, just total classic, looks at Clay and says "Son, were you dropped on your head? When it rains, you just put the windows up! Dumbass."

(He laughs.)

HOMEWORK EATS DOG
AND OTHER WOEFUL TALES

Alan Haehnel

Mr. Kobekeanski loves the morning his big science project is due. The desperate excuses of his students bring him sadistic joy.

MR. K. Good morning. My name is Douglas Kobekeaneski. Since I am now functioning in my official capacity as a high school science teacher, however, you may expunge my first name from your memory. I am Mr. Kobekeaneski. Today is Friday, October 13. Friday the 13th. It is also the day on which a very large, very difficult, very long-term, very potentially grade-devastating assignment is due for my class. On Friday the 13th. Yes, I planned it that way. *(He begins to laugh diabolically, but checks himself.)* I am not cruel, only slightly twisted. It is now 7:28 a.m. I am expecting the first knock on my office door within the next 124 seconds. You see, I have been giving this assignment for the past 23 years, and have come to expect a particular phenomenon on this most weighty of mornings. I call it, affectionately, The Hour of Desperation. *(He begins to laugh diabolically again, but cuts it even shorter.)* Not cruel. Twisted. Before the first bell for school rings, I expect to have a plethora of students coming to me with myriad excuses why they should have an extension on this monolithically important assignment. I look forward to the inventiveness of this hour, the creativity of this hour, and, most of all, the sheer student desperation of this hour! *(One short maniacal chortle, then nothing but a raised eyebrow to remind us—not cruel, just a bit twisted.)* Please be advised that, though the students you are about to see will come with all manner of excuse, I have never, ever, in 23 years, granted a single extension. Not one. *(Knock from offstage.)* Ah! Who ever might that be? Enter!

THE KATRINA PROJECT:
HELL AND HIGH WATER

Michael Marks and Mackenzie Westmoreland

Billy, a high school student, cannot forget the screams during his first night volunteering in New Orleans.

BILLY. I got permission to skip high school for a week to go on a rescue mission in New Orleans. All my teachers required is that I write a report about what I saw and did. Sounds like a good deal, right?

I arrived in New Orleans to the sounds of people screaming for help. But it was too dark and the police wouldn't let us go in. The next morning while boating around the flooded city I saw several children with their heads sticking out of the attic—dead—those were the screams I had heard.

I rescued a woman who handed me a bloody pillowcase. She told me her baby son was in it. That she had given birth to him on a roof and that while she was waiting to be rescued, he died.

I saw dozens of bloated bodies float past my boat. I almost threw up from the smell. I watched many people drown. I saw a girl clinging to a piece of plywood, only to be pushed off by a man trying to save himself. I grabbed her and pulled her into the boat. But when we arrived at the evacuation site I had no choice but to leave her there, even though there were no government officials to release her to and mobs of people fighting over supplies, I wanted to stay with that little girl. She was too small and too weak to take care of herself. *(Pause. Takes bottle of pills from pocket.)* I have to take medication to help me sleep now. I have yet to write that school report. I'm really having a hard time. I know we couldn't save everyone, but I won't ever forget the screaming.

KOCHENDERFER'S FRANKENSTEIN

Tim Kochenderfer

The Creature has just killed the wife of his creator, Victor Frankenstein, on the couples wedding night in revenge for abandoning the Creature. Franken-stein, who had just left to investigate a strange noise outside, runs back to the honeymoon suite after hearing his bride scream.

FRANKENSTEIN. Elizabeth! What is it is… Ah, phew. You're just sleeping. I thought I heard you screaming and something horrible had happened. That crash outside turned out to be nothing. Someone had turned on a wrecking ball and it nailed a car that was driving by sending it flying into a nearby field. I guess that is something. *(Pause.)* I should probably wake you up before talking to you. *(He notices a card next to* ELIZABETH.*)* What's this? *(He picks it up and opens it; reads:)* "On your wedding day…" *(He opens to the inside of the card and reads:)* "All the joy that fills your life, there is none so great as being husband and wife. With love and peace and joy-filled tears, I wish you happiness throughout the years. P.S. I've killed your wife. Love, The Creature!" *(Throws card down.)* Elizabeth!

> *(He shakes her.)*

She is dead! Oh no! No, no, no! That's it! I didn't marry my wife for her to be murdered by my own creation! I married her to seek revenge on my creation. Nobody turns the tables after I have turned the tables. I will find you creature! No matter where you are! *(Glances down.)* What's this? *(He picks up the card and reads:)* "P.P.S., If your pathetic being wishes to find me, simply head north. Love, The Creature." From this point on, my sole purpose in life is to destroy my creation! *(Goes to leave.)* I should probably call police about this murder. There's no time, I'll just pencil a note. *(Picks up paper and writes:)* Dear police, I know this looks like I did this, but I

---

totally didn't. I'll explain later, Victor Frankenstein. That should do just fine. I'm off!

LAW & ORDER: FAIRY TALE UNIT

Jonathan Rand

During the trial against the Big Bad Wolf, a disgruntled and badly bruised police detective H.D. takes the witness stand to provide testimony for the carnivore's crime. Defense attorney Peep challenges H.D., demanding that he reveal the source of his wounds, as it may well render him unfit for testimony.

H.D. All right... You wanna know? Fine. I'll tell you. I'll tell you right now. But don't blame me if you're plagued with nightmares for the rest of your life...

> *(What follows is a highly emotional monologue, as slow and gripping as it needs to be.)*

It was Thursday afternoon. I was on my lunch break. There I was, sitting, minding my own business. But I wasn't sitting just anywhere. No... No I wasn't... I was sitting on a wall. That's right, a wall. It seemed stable enough, sure. Why wouldn't a wall be stable? *(Pause.)* But then out of the blue...without warning...it gave way. Before I could get my bearings, I lost my balance, and... *(Pause.)* ...and I fell.

And it wasn't just your average fall. No it wasn't. It's not easy to describe the kind of the fall it was, but...if I had to choose a word... I'd say it was...great. A great fall. *(Quietly:)* It was great...

I regained consciousness in a gurney over at King's County. They did everything they could to fix my bone fractures, my torn joints, ... my broken soul. All the finest doctors lent a hand—human doctors, of course, but also horse doctors... After surgery...the chief resident put his hoof in my hand and told me everything was gonna be all right.

But he was *all wrong*...

No matter how hard they tried, they failed…they failed at putting me back together again.

You wanna know about my physical stability? Oh I'll be all right. Sure. I'll survive. But after a fall of such…great…magnitude… I may not ever recover…up here. *(Points to his head.)* And in here. *(Points to his heart.)* And along here. *(He indicates the side of his pinky.)*

For those of you out there—you young people, especially—listen to me and listen close… 'Cause I'll only say it once: The next time you see a wall…*respect* that wall… And don't sit on it. Sit on a chair… Or maybe a futon.

    (Pause.)

Happy now?

I quit.

THE LESS THAN HUMAN CLUB

Timothy Mason

Clinton, a model student, complains that he can't satisfy his parent's expectations.

CLINTON. My dad drilled it into us, aim high, aim high, Melissa and me, aim high. Now I tell him I want to go into pre-med, he's furious, you know why? That's too high. Be a vet like me. Is that perfect? From the time I was twelve, he had me memorizing Martin Luther King's speeches, and Davis I am telling you, that man is a fine speaker but he does go on. Mom stepped in on that one, thank God, it's just excerpts now, can you believe it? They won't hardly talk to Julie. Know why? Aimed too low there. See, it's a fine line. That's a human being they're calling low. That's my girl they're calling low. So I start doing some thinking on my own, right? Read up on Elijah Muhammad, there's a group in the city meets once a week, Muslims, Davis, not Lutherans, not Catholics, whatever you are. And at first I think, cool. This is way beyond M.L. King, Junior. And inside of two months, they are on me and on me and on me for going out with a white girl. So where am I? What do I do?

I'm thinking, fuck 'em all. I'm thinking, I'm on my own.

THE LESS THAN HUMAN CLUB

Timothy Mason

Davis, who is gay, attempts to confess to his priest.

DAVIS. Look—can I just skip to what I want to say? My mother's got me going to this shrink because she's afraid maybe I'm not normal. Okay, me too, maybe I'm afraid I'm maybe not normal. But I hate it! This old guy with hairs growing out of his nose and his ears, he keeps talking about his own childhood, like how hard he had it, sole support of about 28 brothers and sisters, and I don't really care, you know? And about healthy thoughts and unhealthy thoughts, but Father, I hate it, I don't feel sick. I don't think I'm sick, I don't know. If I were sick, wouldn't I feel sick? I sort of want to clip the hairs on the end of his nose, maybe that's sick. But I've asked this girl to the next dance you know, and that scares me a little bit. So what I want to know is about the power of prayer and all that. You know?

LUNA PARK

Caridad Svich

Daniel tells a young woman he's just met, a woman he is instantly attracted to and feels a strong rapport with, about the world and life he's come from, the sadness and beauty and roughness of life, and the power of wishing.

DANIEL. I've had friends die. Just like that.

People I saw practically every day, people I hung out with, spent time…routine, right? Nothing you'd think about. And then one day—gone. Wiped out. No reason.

Except hatred. There's lots of that. And that's what I've lived with most of my life.

People all around hating cause that's what they know,

That's how they've been raised.

"Hate that one, he's brown, he talks different."

"Hate the other, he's white, he talks different. Or he believes in a different God."

It's hate all the same. Just a fact. No tears. Cause well… what good are they?

I understand that. Not wanting to cry. Not having to.

Cause you're spent and can't anymore. So, you bury things. Deep down.

You push everything into a little corner in your brain and just forget

cause it feels good to forget everything;

To play *futbol.* Soccer, like you say.

Be in the moment.

Live for the now, and just get on with things.

…But wishing?

It's always there, kicking about in your system, in the metaphysics of it all…

Cause wishing is elemental. Like breathing almost.

You wish for someone to love you.
You wish for someone to be found.
You wish for silly things, stupid things…
Gadgets, games, music,
and then there's
what you wish for
that's totally else…
less tangible things,
impossible things
that you think just by wishing
can be possible.

Like I wish I didn't feel pain. Ever. Impossible, right?
I wish there was a feeling of happiness that could last more than a minute.
I wish everything wasn't such a big deal,
and that we could just talk to each other
without tensing up
and thinking about things we don't want to think about.
Bad memories. Yeah. They flood me. I shrug them off.
That's what I've learnt to do, but it's not what I want.
What I want is
that they would go away
and never come back.
I wish my thoughts wouldn't stray all over the place.
I wish people believed in something and really believed in it
And not just said they did
because it looks good in a newspaper headline.

I wish this park was inside me so I could take it with me wherever I go,
So I could take you with me…
I wish I could go home,
and knew what that meant.
I wish that pool over there smelt of violets instead of chlorine
So we could dip into it and feel the breath of the ancients:
they could give us their wisdom; we could give them our youth.
I wish I could look at you without thinking about my whole life…

LUNA PARK

Caridad Svich

Flaco describes what it was like to survive a bombing in the local park, losing his best friend, and the slow tracing of a day etched in the mind.

FLACO. We were about to dive when there was this noise.
Real loud. Like when the Shock Drop is at max.
Except louder, more abrupt.
I stopped. I looked toward the noise.
When I turned back
He was gone. Just like that. Cory was gone.

The air got thick.
There was dust everywhere.
There was this smell. Like burning hair.
There was a huge cloud of smoke, and an extraordinary silence.
You couldn't hear anything for a long time.
I think there's something really beautiful about things when they get hushed like that.
Like you can feel the earth, the expanse of it...and where you fit in...
And then sirens...slowly. And screams.

Some people were walking with great purpose
Like they wanted to pretend everything was fine
Other people were covered in blood.
I thought I was going to die cause there was so much smoke,
But I'm okay. I'm lucky.
That's the word you heard the most that day
"Lucky. I feel lucky."
It's not a word I like. It feels small, puny. Life should be more than luck.

Now it's just shock, and wondering why...

Who would do such a thing…?
…Seventy dead, two hundred wounded
I don't want vengeance.
I'm just curious. Cause it can't be just hatred, or evil, or craziness
That makes somebody do something like that…
There has to be a legitimate, explain-able reason why someone would think
setting off a bomb is the only solution to solve a problem.

I left the park and started walking.
Each siren that cut the air was followed by absolute silence.
I must've walked miles and miles.
It felt as if I was somewhere else, an unfamiliar place.
Even my language changed. I couldn't really talk to people.
Not cool, you know. There was no flow.
It was all nods, looks, shrugs and hands waving…
But somehow the signs got through…

Rescue workers labored under the yellow glow of arc lights.
I slowly made my way home, far away from the park.
I thought about Cory and how I swore to myself I wouldn't tell anybody
He pitched himself off the cliff.
What good would it do to tell anyone now
that he had said goodbye to the world and all that?
Let them think what they like.
I put on a CD. Morrissey.
The song was "Angel, Angel Down we go together."

OVER THE TAVERN

Tom Dudzick

The year is 1959. 12-year-old Rudy Pazinski rushes into church and kneels in a pew. Oops, he forgot to genuflect. He jumps out of the pew, genuflects quickly and jumps back in. He makes a quick sign of the cross and folds his hands, pointing them to Heaven.

RUDY. Please, please, please Dear Jesus, please make her ease up on me. I promise I'll learn my catechism and get confirmed and all that, but please, I mean, c'mon, look at that! *(Shows the stinging palm of his hand to heaven.)* Please just make her not so mean, that's all. And I'll be a soldier for you, I promise. Whatever that means, I'll do it. Thank you. *(Makes a quick sign of the cross, gets up, then suddenly kneels again.)* And the spaghetti! *(Quick sign of the cross.)* The spaghetti! Please don't let Daddy forget the spaghetti tonight. Please, please, that's very important. The spaghetti. Don't let him forget the spaghetti. Okay? The spaghetti. Very important. So, it's Sister Clarissa and the spaghetti. Thank you.

> *(Makes a quick sign of the cross, gets up, genuflects, almost makes it out, but he runs back again, rushes a genuflection, kneels and makes the sign of the cross.)*

And the bad mood! Ple-e-eze dear Jesus, don't let Daddy be in a bad mood tonight. Please, just no bad mood! Supper would be great without that. No bad mood, please. And I'll learn my catechism and get confirmed. Okay, so it's a nicer Sister Clarissa, the spaghetti, and no bad mood, and I'll get confirmed. Okay, thank you, dear Jesus, thank you!

OVER THE TAVERN

Tom Dudzick

The year is 1959. 12-year-old Rudy Pazinski kneels in a church pew.

RUDY. Jesus, what did you do?! Sister Clarissa's in the hospital! I just asked that you make her ease up on me, I didn't say rub her out! ...And now Daddy's bad mood is worse. And we never did get the spaghetti. Is this a punishment? All 'cause I'm looking for something else? How can you blame me, Jesus? All I get from you is rules. No miracles, no fun, just rules. And crazy rules! Like don't eat meat on Friday. I can't believe you came all the way down to Earth to say that. What's it for? Eddie says you might've done it for the Apostles, to help their fish business. That I could see. But, okay, they're dead now, and I'm still eating fish sticks on Friday. And I hate fish sticks!

And other stuff, like giving up things for Lent. Last year, because you died on the cross, I gave up TV for a month. I'm not complaining. But in the end you came back from the dead, and I saw everything on reruns anyway, so what was the point? ...I've got to keep looking, Jesus. But you understand. I know this kid, Arnie Silverman; I always see him at the Sunday matinees. And he says you switched religions, too. You started out Jewish! And you said it yourself— "Go thou and do likewise!"

SCIENCE FAIR

Jeanmarie Williams

Jethro, a 15-year-old high school "burn-out," presents his science fair project to a panel of judges. He indicates a display of three different broccoli plants, marked "Okay," "Big," and "Dead." He has a violin.

JETHRO. Resolved: if you talk nice to broccoli, it will grow better and produce more vitamins and make it more nutritious. For my experiment, I decided to measure the effect of different qualities of sounds on three broccoli plants. Broccoli, as you know, or maybe not, well, anyway, broccoli contains an electrical charge, which, if stimulated, produces better broccoli. Well, like, you couldn't really make a lamp out of it or anything, I tried that last year, but, okay, if you stimulate it in the right way it will produce bigger florets, more vitamins… Yeah. So, yeah, this is my broccoli.

(He stares out at us.)
(Then he remembers to continue.)

Okay. So here's the thing about it. You should notice that these plants all look different. One is big and healthy, another is just okay and the other one is pretty much dead.

(Again he stares.)

Yeah. So, okay. Here's what I did. I maintained my plants in different rooms. I exposed each of my plants to the same words and tone of voice every day, five times a day. I said different things to each one, but what I said to each individual plant was the same… Yeah, did you get that? Okay, like this is what I said to this one, every day.

(He turns to the dead-looking head of broccoli.)
(JETHRO turns around and prepares his character.)

(He turns around and has taken on the persona of a huge, brutish, mean man.)
(He focuses on the dead broccoli.)
(He drops the character for a moment.)

Okay, so this isn't what I said every day to this one, I mixed it up a little bit, but this is basically the idea.

(He takes on the character again.)

Yooouuu, stupid worthless piece of crap! You dumbass piece of fiber! Who'd want to eat you anyway? What are you, *green*? Are you green? God damn the day you were born! Die! Die! Die! So, yeah, so this one's dead. And…this is what I said to this one: *(He turns to the "okay" looking broccoli.)* Get on Route 7. When you hit the Grove Street exit, get in the right lane and bear right at the yield sign. It's a tough merge, so watch out you don't change lanes. At the Mobil station, turn right. Go through three lights and the high school is on your left hand side, just past the Wal-Mart.
This one grew, but it's, you know, just okay. So you got that. Yeah. And so this is what I said to this one.

(He indicates the one marked "Big." It looks beautiful and healthy.)
(He takes out his violin and plays to the plant. It's rather beautiful. He stops and looks at us.)

SPLIT

Allison Moore

Jake, 23, a middle-distance runner trying to make the big time. He is running better than he ever has in his life. His words are like his motion: explosive, joyous and very fast.

JAKE. When I run I see out the back of my head
In front of me, behind me
Supersonic x-ray vision bubble and I'm running right in the middle
of it.
You think I'm lying, talking smack
I am telling you how it IS.
The sensation of the air moving over my skin
The sound of the runner coming up behind me
The rate at which that sound has to travel
to catch up with me at my blazing fast pace
Every moment every sensation is taken in
Analyzed and reanalyzed
in a split second
not in my brain
in my body.
The proprioceptors
PRO-PRE-O-CEPTORS
Working all the time
clickety-clickety like a film.
Each picture shows me where I am
and the faster you move, the more frames you get.
THIS is how you see out the back of your head.
THIS is how you know where your opponent is at all times,
and KNOW, Does he have a fifth gear, sixth gear?
Fuck Superman.
Motion is Kryptonite.

SPRING

Tanya Palmer

Michael, the class valedictorian, reads the first draft of his speech to the teaching staff—it's not quite what they had expected.

MICHAEL. Great, okay, well here it goes. It's a little rough still, I'll fix it up, and make it more formal for the real thing.

Ladies and Gentlemen, Fellow Students, teachers, parents. I've been given the honor and responsibility of speaking to you on this very important day. Graduation. We, your sons and daughters, students, friends, we are embarking on a new phase of our lives, our journey into the 'real world.' As always, when beginning on a new path, it is a chance to not only look forward into the future, but also to look back, at what you've learned and who you've become. Well, these are some of my thoughts on what I've learned as a student. I've learned that we sit all day, being fed information that somebody decided was important. I've learned that we spend our days and nights, thinking about ideas that have almost no meaning in our everyday lives. I've learned that we are taught to pretend, who we are, what we want, what we think, but that we should never be real, never express our real desires, our fears, our fantasies, cause that would be wrong. Inappropriate. I've learned that the rules are just there so the teachers can have their coffee breaks undisturbed. I've learned to be polite and clean, to say the right thing, to have the right opinions and the right goals. I've learned that all that history, math and literature is there to help us pretend, to create the illusion that we're more than we really are. We're just bodies, you know? You like to pretend like we're these floating heads with grand ideas capable of altering the planet. But slowly, all these empty ideas and meaningless rules are sucking the life out of us, making us into these puppets moving through hallways, listening for bells to ring so we know when to eat, when to leave, waiting for someone to tell us what to read, what to say, we keep moving, learning more useless information, talking more bullshit, till we're just corpses, our mouths moving but nothing coming out. I watch you people, my teachers, my parents, my friends, staring ahead with blank eyes, speaking in voices that are not your own. Dead people. People spend their lives worrying about what's right, what they should do…and you know what? It kills them. I think it takes more courage to take a shotgun, stick it in your mouth and blow your brains out, then it does to go on and on, living a life that makes you miserable. Let's stop pretending. Set aside the empty words, the bullshit information, the rules telling us who we're supposed to be. Become who you are. Creatures of instinct. Do what you're not supposed to do. Grab at what you want. Kill your enemy. Destroy yourself if that's what it takes. Cause that's all we've got are our bodies. Our desires. That's all we are. Animals. Animals with a taste of blood.

So. What do you think?

SQUARE ONE

Mark D. Kaufmann

Darren is the coolest Senior in his High School—until he wakes up one morning in the body of a lowly Freshman. After days of living a twilight zone nightmare, he finds he's still running for student body president against his ex-best friend, and has to deliver his campaign speech to the school assembly. It's not what he planned…

> *(DARREN takes a moment, looking over the school assembly. He is very calm and mature, taking his time with his speech.)*

DARREN. A couple days ago I knew exactly what I'd say up here. I figured you'd want to elect the coolest guy. The guy nothing bothers. The guy with attitude. That's who always wins elections. And he's always a Senior. *(Beat.)* And you probably still want to vote for that guy. But things happened overnight. And…I'm learning being a Senior isn't the only thing…

> *(Darren's attitude takes a sharp and immediate turn from wisdom and humility to outrage and anger:)*

…It's EVERYTHING! Being a Freshman totally sucks the mop! It blows! The Seniors get it all: respect, girls, primo cafeteria tables. Get a clue, people: who wouldn't want that? Anybody who's tasted the Senior world would sell their right arm to have it. And I've seen it—people, you got NO IDEA.

A friend just told me I gotta be what I am; you know what, he's right. Under the skin of this "Freshman" is the coolest Senior you've ever known. That's right. The rules are about to change. You think putting in three long years is the only requirement to really be a Senior? "Senior" is what ya call a state of mind. *(Pointing to a Senior:)* You think *he's* cool? Lemme tell you something: he's more a Freshman than I am. He tells everybody he's taking his time applying to colleges? The guy's got fifteen applications out there

---

already. —Not only that, he actually writes different essays for *each one!* Sounds to me he's kinda eager-beavery—kinda workin' real hard. Is that your definition of a Senior? People, inside that haircut and attitude beats the heart of a Freshman of gargantuan proportions.

And he ain't alone. Look at who's sittin' next to you. You think you know what class they really belong in? You think you got 'em pegged? You don't know jack. *(Beat.)* Look: you guys do what you want; I don't give a rat's ass. But you want cool? You want the definition of "Senior"? You talk to me.

STRESS, PRESSURE, DOOM AND OTHER TEEN DELIGHTS

Alan Haehnel

Jack expresses the extreme pressure he is under as the latest in a long line of prestigious college-attenders.

JACK. Can I help it that I am surrounded by collegiate geniuses? I mean, is it my fault that I'm feeling this pressure that's so amazing that I can barely even function? I don't just feel the weight of my parents' expectations—oh, no. I come from at least five generations of college-going people, on both sides of the family. You know who's got it made? Doug Madson—he's going to be the first in his family to go to college. That's all he's got to do—just go. Podunk U., Two-Year Tech., College of St. Ralph of the Holy Ant Farms…it doesn't matter where he goes—he just has to go somewhere! Now that's luxury.

Look at what I'm up against. What do you expect?

You got your great-great-uncle who graduated top of his class from Harvard and invented a revolutionary new cure for foot fungus. You got your 26 class presidents, 18 class vice-presidents, 32 class secretaries and the longest running mascot in the history of Yale, who actually died in his mascot suit at the age of 88.

You've got this uncle and that aunt and this cousin and that godfather all whispering in your ear, "Oh, don't go there; go here." "Oh, skip there; this is the best place." "Oh, I wouldn't be caught dead there; this college will really launch your career." And the whole time, hovering over it all, in your mind, you've got this picture of your long-gone distant relative lying dead from exhaustion inside a bulldog suit!

TESTING, TESTING

Alan Haehnel

Scott only needs to pass this one test so he can graduate and go into the military. He pleads for help from his classmates.

SCOTT. What is the big deal? I have laughed with you people. I have partied with you people. I have lived in this stupid building for the past 12 years with you people. I need somebody's help. If I saw any of you in trouble, I would be there, don't you know that? So why won't somebody help me?

People cheat every day. People cheat to get money, to…get ahead. I'm asking you to help me. It means that you, Mr. Captain of the Soccer team, Mr. Class president, Mr. A student, Mr. son of the richest guy in town, Mr. Mercedes, you can afford all the honor you want. It's no skin off your back. You try being me. Honor's easy when you've got everything going for you, man. When you're on the right side of the people setting up the code, honor's easy.

But what if you don't have the brains or the athletics or the looks or the money…all the advantages? What if your old man is a drunk and your mother has to work three jobs and she still ain't got enough, huh, rich boy? It's not a pity party! It's the truth! How many of you have gone home to find every piece of furniture in the house smashed to pieces, huh? Smashed to bits because your father owed some crook money and that crook broke into your house and destroyed every piece of furniture?

THANK YOU FOR FLUSHING MY HEAD IN THE TOILET, AND OTHER RARELY USED EXPRESSIONS

Jonathan Dorf

Fresh from having his head flushed in a toilet by a bully, Achilles fantasizes about what it would be like to launch the perfect counterattack.

ACHILLES. That's how it goes in my mind. He shoves my head in the bowl, flushes, and I pop up, jack in the box: thank you!

(Beat.)

The problem is that in real life, I never get past choking on the bowl water. My brain is trying to say "thank you," and the rest of me is gagging, and if the toilet wasn't flushed before I—let's not even go there.

(Beat.)

Since "thank you" doesn't seem to be happening, I'm working on another strategy: vomiting. I'm optimistic about vomiting, because it's all I can do not to vomit already, so this would be like going with the flow, and even better: his legs are right there.

(Demonstrates by getting on his knees and swiveling to one side.)

It's just point and shoot. And if you knew that every time you gave me a swirly you were gonna have to go home and change your pants, you'd think twice. It's the power of retaliatory vomiting.

(Beat.)

And that's just the beginning. They say that the best defense is a good offense, which is why I'm taking it to the next level: preemptive vomiting.

(Beat. "Four o'clock" in the next line means the location, not the time.)

Trouble at four o'clock. Fire projectiles on my mark.

(Feigns vomiting.)

We've got on 'em on the run. I repeat. The enemy is in full retreat.

(Beat.)

I hate vomiting. It's the worst feeling in the world. Almost as bad as having your head stuck in a flushing toilet.

THE WHY

Victor Kaufold

Robert, a teenager, is speaking with a prison therapist after having perpetrated a school shooting.

ROBERT. Yeah. People in cars are…funny. It's like…they're exaggerations of what they're like in the real world. They're in this car, and it's like they're completely absorbed in their own little capsule. Nothing outside of the car matters unless it's going to affect their car. They just sit there completely focused on the red light waiting for it to turn green. I'm pretty sure the wish "man, I hope this light turns green soon" is thought more often than "man, I wish everyone on Earth could live together in peace." —Traffic light was invented by a black man. Did you know that?

Well, some people, they're so wrapped up in their little car related affairs, they don't notice anything. —Even things that are car universe relevant, like, say, the light changing. Then, this of course sends the guy behind them, who seemed fine just one second ago, into a complete and total rage. And you can watch him go out of his mind and wave his arms around inside his little capsule. —And during this special period, a person could do any of a number of things to this upstanding citizen, and he would never be the wiser.

But I've forgotten the best part: The people who do notice me, but *pretend* not to. Those are by far the coolest. You know, I'll start doing something weird, and they'll notice,—but instantly, this reflex kicks in which tells them not to look. So they just try to sit there and get nervous because they realize that their capsule is in danger of collapsing. But then, the black man's invention turns green, and they're off, safe and never to be seen again. One out of every million people will notice me, but they're usually kids, and kids of course don't count.

THE WIZARD OF OZ

adapted by Erin Detrick
from the book by L. Frank Baum

*Having just had his joints oiled by the Scarecrow, the Tin Woodman explains
how he found himself in this predicament.*

TIN WOODMAN. I know—it's coming out wrong. A little more
oil, please? Thank you.

I learned to be a wood-chopper from my father, and when I was
grown, I fell in love with a beautiful Munchkin girl, who loved me
back. What bliss it was to feel love. But she lived with an old
woman who wanted to keep the girl all to herself so that she'd always have someone to cook and clean for her. When the old
woman learned of my intentions, she asked the Wicked Witch of
the East to prevent the marriage. The Wicked Witch enchanted my
ax, and as I was chopping logs for our house, the axe slipped and
chopped off my leg.

I went to a tin-smith, and he fixed me a nice new one. This angered
the Witch, and so when I began chopping again, my axe slipped
and cut off my other leg. I had a new one made, and then the axe
chopped off first one arm, then the other, then it chopped me
clean in two.

The tin-smith fixed me every time, but I'd lost my heart, and so I
no longer cared whether or not I married the Munchkin girl. She
might still be waiting for me, but without a heart, what can I do?

So, I no longer worried about cutting myself, but I had to be
careful to always keep an oil can nearby. One day I was so busy
chopping I didn't notice the clouds darkening, and I didn't think to
stop as the rain started plopping down. By the time I noticed it was
too late. I had many months to think about what I had lost, and re-

solved that if I could only get a heart, I could know love again and be happy, because I was never so happy as when I was in love.

Female

THE 1ST ANNUAL ACHADAMEE AWARDS
(full-length version)

Alan Haehnel

Connie is nominated as the best female actor (liar) at Achadamee High School. This monologue shows her at work.

CONNIE. Mom, please sit down. Listen, I know you've been disappointed with my behavior in the past. I haven't always made wise choices. When I had Bill Raymond drive his motorcycle into our living room, that was a bad choice. When I shoplifted those times, those were bad choices, especially when I set up my on-line clothing business with the stolen goods and made over sixteen thousand dollars selling brand-name items for a significant discount. I shouldn't have done that. The thing with the explosives and the police breaking through our windows at two in the morning, that was wrong. I can see that now. But Mom, I need you to know that I have changed. I truly have. I am not the same girl I was last week when I tried to market my unique brand of cigarettes. You can believe me now. You can trust me. Please. I am a changed person. I am back to being that innocent, trust-worthy little girl you sent off to kindergarten so many years ago. So when I ask you if I can borrow our new Jetta for the next week and a half, and to completely disregard that odd chemical smell coming from the trunk, you can believe me now. I will not let you down.

18 MORE REASONS NOT TO BE IN A PLAY

Alan Haehnel

High-strung Julie tells us one of the 18 Reasons why being in a play is a dangerous idea. At monologue's end, she faints.

JULIE. Because you're a fast talker. You come from a family of fast talkers and if there's such a thing as a gene for fast talking you have definitely inherited it and if you were in a play you'd memorize your lines and all that but you'd say them too fast and you know the director would say…

Take it slower.

And you'd know you're supposed to take is slower and you would say to yourself over and over, "Talk slower, talk slower," but when you worried about it you'd get tense and when you got tense you'd talk even faster so the director would start to get mad and he'd say…

You have to talk slower!

And you'd practically be screaming at yourself inside yourself and beating yourself up because you'd know you were still talking too fast but you'd be getting so nervous about it you'd be getting faster and faster so the director would lose his patience finally and yell…

Slower!

And that would make you go so fast that you never even took a breath and you'd go and go and go and go and go and go so fast that you ran completely out of air but still you'd be telling yourself to slow down so the director wouldn't yell at you because you hated that but you couldn't stop racing and racing until finally you just…

30 REASONS NOT TO BE IN A PLAY

Alan Haehnel

Ostensibly shy Cecily warns us why we should avoid being in a play.

CECILY. Because you're just, you're just, you're just too shy. You...you can barely get two words out of your mouth in front, in front of, of an audience. Whenever you have oral presentations in class, you, you, you, you just take a zero. If somebody tries to force you, you start to cry. A play? Oh, no, no, no. You're painfully shy. That would kill you. You would just die from embarrassment, staring out at those lights, knowing that people are sitting there, judging you—judging what you're wearing, what you're saying, the way you're standing. You'd be mortified! I mean, it's a completely unreasonable request, to ask you to be in a play. They might as well tell you to stand against the wall so they can assemble a firing squad and have you shot, right? You're shy, remember? Hands-freezing, armpits-dripping, knees-knocking, head-pounding shy! Is that a problem? Is it? Just because you're shy, can't you be allowed to just stay in a corner and be that way, or does this society absolutely require that, no matter how traumatic it might be, you have to get up on stage and do whatever some script requires? You're shy, darn it! Shy, shy, shy! So what, if the script says sing the ABC's like an opera star, do you have to go ahead and start singing away? *(Singing like an opera star:)* A-B-C-D-E-F-G! That's way too much to ask of a shy person, I'm telling you! If the script should require that you grab some strange guy *(She grabs a boy and interacts with him through this next segment:)* and hold him close to you like he's your favorite teddy bear; if it commands that you stroke his hair and grab his shirt as if you can't live without him...are you supposed to just go ahead and do that? No! You're too shy! If they script calls for you to kiss him passionately... *(She moves as if she is going to do that. The boy breaks away.)*

You see! He's too shy for that and so are you! You can't be in a play and you can't sing opera and you can't grope some guy and you just can't possibly make a fool of yourself in front of a crowd full of people because *(Screaming, emphasizing every word with huge energy:)* YOU ARE JUST WAY TOO AMAZINGLY, INCREDIBLY, PITIFULLY... *(Suddenly pausing, realizing the irony, and backing off to a whisper:)* ...shy.

30 Reasons Not To Be in a Play
Alan Haehnel

Kim relates her cautionary tale as yet another reason not to be in a play.

KIM. Because if you're in a play, when the play is over, they'll want to have a cast party, which is okay, except that it will be at this boy named Peter's house who you find fairly attractive which is okay except that sometimes when you look at the shape of his face and the depth of his dimples you start to wonder about the names and genders of the offspring you might produce together which is okay except that he has no idea you have a crush on him which is okay except that at the cast party at his house, Peter's mother is going to make this pink, fluffy salad sort of stuff with Cool Whip and strawberry Jell-O and canned fruit cocktail in it which is okay except that when you were four-years-old you sort of loved the stuff so much that you sneaked a huge bowl of it off the buffet table one New Year's Eve and sat under the table with the bowl and a soup spoon and by the time your parents finally found you, you had pretty much o.d.-ed on the stuff which is okay except now every time you even look at the pink fluffy stuff you get that pukey feeling which is okay except at the cast party somebody will put a big mound of the stuff with little bits of fruit poking out of it like body parts in a zombie movie and they'll hold it right up to your face, right under your nose, and they'll say, "Don't you just loooove this pink fluffy stuff?" which is okay except not only will you get that pukey feeling but you'll actually know you're about to worship the porcelain god which is okay but before you can sprint to the bathroom who will end up right in your path but your future husband for all time and eternity, Peter, who will be about to smile and show you his dimples when you'll suddenly make that horrible "raaalph!" noise and you'll vomit all over the brand-new jet black Converse All Stars he bought just for the party. And *that* will definitely *not* be okay!

AT THE BOTTOM OF LAKE MISSOULA

Ed Monk

Pam is a sophomore at a college where she has transferred after her family is killed. She is talking to Jim, another student who has noticed she is in pain but doesn't know why, he has just asked if she needs help. Just before she saw her family for the last time, Pam's sister asked if she could borrow Pam's CD player.

PAM. You want to help me!? OK, you can help me! My whole family was killed by a tornado four months ago. My Mom, my Dad, my brother and sister and the baby. All dead. *(With self-loathing.)* And I wasn't there, cause I needed some peace and quiet. I didn't want to spend an extra *day* with them. So here I am, I got all the money I'll ever need and all I do is spend all day in stupid classes learning useless information. I don't know why I keep going, I guess I'm hoping I can learn something to make sense of it. But there's nothing, it's all the same, it's junk and a bunch of noise …And…I pray and I…I don't know…I have this bottle of sleeping pills they gave me after it happened, and every night I can't get to sleep and I sit there and think about taking the whole bottle. But that's a sin, isn't it? Isn't it? So I can't do that and I don't know what to do. And I'm going crazy, I can't stop thinking about them, everywhere I go, something reminds me of them. Why the hell couldn't I have let her have that damn CD player!?… That's the last thing I ever said to her… So you want to help? Go ahead and help. You tell me what to do. You tell me what to do!

THE BIRDS: A MODERN ADAPTATION

Don Zolidis

Employed by Olympus as a messenger and forced to use a rainbow as a symbol, the teenage goddess Iris has a really hard immortal existence. Here, she rants to anyone who will listen about how much she hates her lame worshippers.

IRIS. Misery. Agony. Life is unending torment. I hate the clothes at the Gap this year. I went over to Apollo's mansion last night— he is so hot—but he doesn't want anything to do with me cause he says I'm too young for him—I'm 347 years old, I don't understand why I gotta be treated like a kid. If he knew the real me I know he'd like me, but he's too busy chasing after Aphrodite, who doesn't even know he exists, and she's just a cow anyway, you shoulda seen the shirt she was wearing yesterday, it was gross, boobs popping out everywhere, like "Oh, look at my chest, I'm the goddess of cleavage." I hate her. Bending over all the time. Slut.

I wish I was the goddess of something cool like volcanoes or skateboarding. Maybe then Apollo would like me. I hate my life. It sucks that I'm immortal. I wish everyone else would die. But they can't cause they're immortal too.

I don't even have cool worshippers. My high priest is this dork named Andrew, which is a lame name if you ask me, and he's all, "Iris, Iris, let me worship you" and I'm like, "Ewww, get away." Last night he sacrificed a sheep just to get my attention and I'm like, desperate much? I don't even like sheep. So I cursed him with all these boils all over his face to show I was pissed off and every- thing, so he sacrificed another sheep. So then I made him go blind and he walked off a cliff which was kind of cool, but then I felt bad about it cause my dad was like, "You're not supposed to kill your priests," and I was like, "I didn't kill him, I just blinded him and he fell off the cliff on his own. I can't be responsible for that." But then I felt bad so I went to Hades and I'm like, "Can I have my priest back?" And Hades was like okay as long as you give me the souls of the first-born of a dozen of your worshippers, so I'm like, fine, whatever, so now, I got Andrew back. But now he's like horribly disfigured from the fall where all the rocks hit his head on the way down and he still has all the boils and he's still blind, and he's supposed to be my earthly representative, right? And now he thinks I've raised him from the dead, so now he thinks he's gotta sacrifice a whole herd of sheep, and I'm like, enough with the sheep! Except now he can't even find the sheep cause he's just stumbling around in the field, so they're just sitting there laughing and baaing at him as he walks around with all these broken bones cause Hades didn't bother fixing him up at all, you know, so he's got one arm that's like pulverized and it's hanging limp from his shoulder and meanwhile there's like no worshippers at my temple, cause this 'tard's there, moaning in pain and drooling all over himself, but he's still got enough sense to say, "Iris! Iris! Iris! I love you, ah! It hurts! The pain! Help me!" blah blah blah blah blah!

So then, just for kicks, Hephaestus curses my priest with immortality. Just to piss me off. So now I can't even kill him.

BLASTER

Victoria Stewart

Cynthia, a punky and self-assured high school student, gives a report on her favorite topic—computer hacking.

CYNTHIA. *(With a smirk:)* "The first rule of Fight Club is, you do not talk about Fight Club." But since I want a good grade and everything I say can be found on the web, I think I'm safe.

The term "hacker" at first just referred to someone with mastery in computers. At MIT in the 50s and 60s, hackers figured out the phone system and railroad switches. They were celebrated for their work and had the support of major universities. In 1969, a blind college student, Joe Engrassia, realized he could whistle a perfect 2600 cycle tone into a phone line and get free long distance. Phreaking, the term for hacking into the telephone system, was born.

In 1971, the Homebrew Computer Club published an article about how to build "Blue Boxes" that could make that tone so that anyone could "phreak" if they wanted. This, by the way, was illegal. These Homebrew guys wanted everyone to have access to computers, because up until then, only universities and the military had them. Two of these guys, Steve Wozniak and Steve Jobs, started Apple Computers and Bill Gates built Microsoft and yeah, surprise, surprise, once they started making money, it was all about the "rights of ownership" rather than the free access to information that they were all about when they started.

In the 1980s, suddenly, there started to be a lot of laws against hacking, including going into a system without the "authority" to do so, even if you didn't break anything.

Let me tell you something.

Most hackers are not trying to "bring down the system." Most hackers just want to see how things work. They just want to *explore*.

Here's a quaint, 1950s way to look at it. In the old days, kids would break into the old abandoned house at the end of the block.

Maybe you just wanted some privacy, a place to be, alone and away from the expectations of your parents.

Or maybe it was the closest thing to being someplace new. What's inside? How do other people live? And as long as you didn't break or steal anything, you'd get a slap on the wrist.

That's what we're doing. We're just tip-toeing through Boo Radley's house.

So leave us alone.

Thank you.

(She curtsies, ironically.)

CIRCUMVENTION

Anton Dudley

Moments before telling her best friend that she is backing out of the class trip to Mexico, Anna (17), takes a private moment to understand her fears. Strangely, she has just taken a bath with an underwater camera and a mermaid doll.

ANNA. Don't laugh at me. I still play with dolls. Not lots of dolls or stuffed animals or anything but. Just this one.

> *(She reveals, from behind her back, a Barbie-sized mermaid doll, which she clutches in her hand.)*

She's not like any of my other dolls. Partly because I don't really have any anymore. But when I got rid of them, around the time I started high school, I kept this one. I don't really know why. I never played with her all that much when I was younger. She wasn't very pretty, I thought. Because of her long leathery tail; she never fit in at the doll tea table, or in the doll SUV, and she couldn't wear ball gowns, and she never got any looks from the Kens or my brother's GI Joes. I mean, can you imagine what their children would have looked like? And I didn't spend much time with her, because, she isn't very soft. Sure, she's got the long, brushable hair, but…that tail and, her skin. Her cold porcelain skin. And she never seemed very happy. Her face was always sort of tight and unwelcoming. Probably because she always wanted to be in the water.

I hate the water. I'm terrified of it.

I live in one of those states: American, not mental: that doesn't touch the ocean. And I'd be lying if I said I didn't feel it: this feeling of being locked in. Locked up. But somehow that's safe, isn't it? Not like the ocean.

It's the big unknown right? The ocean. The seven seas. It's all just a death waiting to happen. And what's worse, to enter this world, this world of water, you have to be practically naked. Vulnerable. And it's dark and strange, full of all these things, and, of course, it won't let you breathe. You gotta hold your breath, close your eyes, swim as fast as you can and hope you make it to…to where? I don't know, the other side? You just got to hold your breath and race as fast as you can in hopes that you make it out alive? Well. When I put it that way, the ocean's a lot like high school. Hm.

Anyway, I didn't get rid of her, for some reason, whatever reason.

Some days I stay home from school. On the days when I do this, I like to take pictures of her in the bathtub. Underwater. It sounds crazy, I know, but…for some reason, whatever reason, I like to take pictures of myself and her together underwater. It's the closest I ever come to being brave.

CLEVELAND

Mac Wellman

Daughter, writing in her diary, fears that she will not be asked to the prom by the right boy.

DAUGHTER. Dear Diary. I feel like I'm losing my mind. Like Losin' Susan. I feel sure Johnny will ask me to the Prom. Johnny on the Spot. If not him, then Panda Hands. I will end it all if he does. I do not wish to go to the Prom because since we have lost all our money we are no longer fashionable. As we once were. Ahead lies a life of meaningless drudgery and not the glitter and champagne of high society. Sigh. I do not love Johnny. But I do love Jimmy. In my secret heart of hearts. Sigh. Jimmy the door. Way to my dreams. I'm not sure I want that. My dreams scare me… Jimmy goes to the Boys Prep School and I go to the Catholic Girls School. Our Lady of the Bleeding Knuckle. Our Lady of the Runny Nose. A chasm of religion divides us. And he will not ask me to the Prom. Yes, because I am not fashionable. If Mother could read this she would know, yes, all my unclean thoughts. To tell the truth, dear diary, I feel quite fed up with life since Dad died and did not go to Heaven. Strange things are afoot in the heavens.

CONSPICUOUS

Winter Miller

Diana, an adoptee, explains how grateful she is for the love and attention of her gay fathers, even if they don't always make her already awkward transition into womanhood any easier.

DIANA. Thank you for inviting me to talk about my experiences as the adopted daughter of gay parents. My fathers Alan and Ricky have provided me with lots of emotional support plus the basics: good clothes and a home. Nobody ever asks is *that* one your father—because I'm black and they're not. I've never looked like anyone. I used to look in magazines or on tv for my relatives. I thought I was related to Will Smith, because we kind of looked alike, I told this girl at camp he's my cousin and she believed me. I feel that family is something people make together, it's not defined by what kind of people are in it… The one thing I would say that is a drawback is they don't understand some girl things. Like, they have no concept of how expensive bras are. Alan hands me twenty bucks and he's all, "get yourself some bras." I'm like, this will only buy half a bra! And he's like, "don't buy the most expensive kind!" So I bring him to Victoria's Secret to show him. Huge mistake. He thinks it's funny to put a bra on over his shirt. People stare. The security guard comes over. That was our last time bra shopping. He still thinks they only cost ten dollars! Oh, also, they cannot be trusted to buy the right maxi pads. They put all the brands on the floor and compare shop! "You get 24 for this price"—"but look these have wings on them!" "Wheee! Wings!" "But these you can wear for days…" For days? Who wears a maxi pad for days?? I'm sure all dads are not like that, but some sensitivity training is in order. They tried to talk to me about sex but I was all, we have health class for this and I can ask friends or their moms. Ricky has done my hair since I had hair, so he's pretty good. He said I could get dreads, but he would miss our girl bonding time. They can be annoying, but that's common. I would like to know what my mom was like—but my parents can't change that. I got very lucky with my dads. Check with me in ten years, maybe I'll have a different answer, but I doubt it. Thank you.

DRACULA

Mac Wellman

Lucy confesses to her friend Mina how she came to be alone, above the sea, and bitten.

LUCY. It all seemed quite real, for I knew I was not dreaming. I only wanted to be at this particular spot—I don't know why, for I was afraid of something—I don't know what. I do know I wanted to do something; something very very bad. I remember, though I suppose I was asleep, passing through the streets and over the bridge. A fish leaped as I passed by. And I heard a lot of dogs barking and howling, all barking at once, as I went up the steps. Then I had a vague memory of something long and dark with red eyes; and something very sweet and very bitter all around me at once; and then I seemed to be sinking into deep green water, and there was a singing in my ears, as I have heard there is to drowning men. My soul seemed to go out from my body and float about in the air. I seem to remember that, for a time, the West lighthouse was underneath, as if I had been thrown into the air. All I wanted was to be with you and Jack and Quincey and dear Professor Van Helsing. And then I came back and found you shaking my body. I saw you do it before I felt you.

ELOISE & RAY

Stephanie Fleischmann

Eloise, 16, relives the moment when she told her best friend Rosanna about losing her virginity with her sweetheart Ray.

ELOISE. I said to Rosanna. "Him and me, we— He devirginized me. Yesterday. I am now de." And she said, "Congratulations. From this moment on, in honor of this, I will call you DeVee."
And I said, "Not around my Daddy, you won't."
"That's right," she said. "He would KILL you if he found out. But MY lips are zipped."
And then she looked at me and she looked at me for the longest time, and I said, "What are you staring at?"
And she said, "I'm trying to see if you look different."
"Do I?" I said. "Do I look different?"
And she said, "No. You look like Eloise. You look like you always did. Do you feel like her?"
"Her?" I said.
"Eloise," she said. "Same old same old."
"But the same old same old feels different every day," I said.
Seethrough.
"You know what I mean," she said.
And so I told her: "I do. I feel different."
Glow in the dark.
"I feel like I am his and he is mine and he will never leave me. He will never let me go."
"Well that's a cliché if I ever heard one," said Rosanna.
"But I do," I said, "I feel different. I feel a changing— I am the me that was always meant to be."
"You be careful," said Rosanna. "That's a dangerous business."
"You wanna know how I really feel?" I said.

"I feel like an oyster. All this time I been an oyster, and I never even knew it. All this time takin in sand and takin in sand and it's been workin on me, workin inside me to make this— This pearl. Only it took him to pry me open and pick it out."

FASHIONISTAS

Janet Allard

Echo speaks freely—without echoing anyone—for the first time in her life. She mourns the death of her love, Narcissus.

ECHO. He disappeared.
Transformed.
He was cut off in the flower of his youth.

(She shows the flower around to the crowd.)

I found this, where he had been.
Where I saw him
leaning into the pool
Like a statue carved out of Parisian marble
He hovered on the brink
Fascinated. Gazing.
Drowning in his own image
Spellbound by himself.
He got lost.
He tried and tried.
But he could not grab hold of himself. (Lay hold upon himself.)
He realized what he loved was in image a reflection.
Wasn't even real.
And when he couldn't bear it anymore.
As golden wax melts with gentle heat
As morning frost melts with the sun
He wasted away with love
He was consumed by its fire
He drowned in its depths
Until nothing remained of the body we loved

His eyes were twin stars.
Everything bright and shining and better than life.

(ECHO *puts the flower down.*)

A FREE MAN IN PARIS

Brooke Berman

Isa, a teenager living with her terminally ill mother, takes a drive with her best friend.

ISA. Parents are so random. Parents are like, "But where are you going?" I mean, my mom can be great. She was really great a lot when I was...you know. Before she was...you know. But I mean now she's like... I don't know, she can be great. But she can also be like this totally false being, just pretending to be whatever she thinks a Parent is. And the thing is, she's completely spaced out and self involved. But then, like she checks into The Parent Thing, and she's a mess. Like, things with—you know, her health, whatever—get bad, and she kinda forgets about me for a while. And then, she remembers she's a mom. And this is when you don't want to be around. Because once she remembers, she has to do something to makes herself feel like a mom. And so then, she does these totally random things. Like, she starts asking about where I'm going or what I do or if I'm fucking smoking pot or something. Because she read somewhere that kids use Visine when they're trying to hide that they're using drugs and I have Visine, so therefore, I'm probably like on crack. Which is fucking absurd if you know me at all. Which is EXACTLY the point because clearly she doesn't. I mean, that whole generation is just not okay.

Her concern is ridiculous and random and totally unwarranted. I take care of myself. I take care of her. I take care of you. Everyone is taken care of. But my mom, she's all "Where are you going?".

GORGEOUS RAPTORS

Lucy Alibar-Harrison

Kaballah, a sixteen-year-old high school outcast, escapes her life through an ongoing fantasy about being a dinosaur. Here we see Kaballah's entrance into her fantasy world for the first time. Her eyes are closed in a rapture of Raptor-dom.

KABALLAH. It's morning in Pangea. An azure mist rises up out of the ferns and subtly blends with the scarlet hues of—burgeoning sun. Raptor rises.

(KABALLAH rises slightly from her crouch.)

She surveys the sparse and chlorinated landscape. Awwwwk! A danger has been spotted in Raptor's midst! She flexes her razor sharp claws and stiffens her wings. Her immaculate eyesight focuses in on—oh, God! It's a Testosteronous Pimple Beast! This is but a temporary problem. Bum-ba-da-duuuum. With one fell swoop, Raptor is upon him. "Ahhhh! Ahhh! Curse you, Raptor!" But Raptor only cackles. "Awwwk-awwk-awwk-awwk!" She buries her beak into the navel of the Testosternous Pimple Beast and sucks up his intestines like twinkie filling! "Ssssssssk."

(To audience.)

Mmmm! He had chicken for lunch!

The rest of the body is soon to follow, oozing grease all the way down. Just how Raptor likes it. The landscape is once again desolate. Her belly is full of Testosternous Pimple Beast. Raptor arches her back and emits a Raptor cry of triumph. "Awwwwk!" She spreads her wings and soars, clean and free, into the scarlet horizon.

JENNA AND HER PRIZE-WINNING PIG CHANGE THE COURSE OF HISTORY

Dwayne Yancey

Ashley, an ambitious TV reporter in a small town, complains about being stuck covering a county fair. The assignment stinks. Literally.

TV REPORTER ASHLEY. *(On a cell phone:)* …and you would not believe what they have me doing today! The fair! That's right, the county fair! I swear, when I get home tonight I'm going to have to wash my hair in tomato juice just to get the animal odors out of it. This place stinks like a barnyard! Well, I guess that's because it is a barnyard. They've got pigs, and goats and sheep and who knows what all some of the animals are. And my shoes are already, yuck, I don't want to talk about my shoes. I tell you, this place is right out of "Hee Haw"! I can't believe this! Four years of college, two internships, and I wind up working for the farm report! Hang on, I've got another call coming in, that might be my news director. I'll get right back to you. Channel 3 Action News, Ashley Fairweather speaking—oh, hello, yes, oh, I'm here all right. No, there's nothing going on that I can tell, just some silly livestock judging contest thing with kids. What? You're putting me on? No way. You can't be serious! A live shot? At five? You mean I've got to stick around that long? Geez, that's forever. Yeah, yeah, I know it's the top-rated show at that hour, but you don't understand! This is the county fair! It stinks! No, I don't mean it's a bad assignment, well, yes, I do mean it's a bad assignment. I mean, it stinks! It really stinks! It smells! It's all icky, and I've got something on my shoes and I don't even want to think about what it might be. I don't care if they are cute kids. They're farm kids. They probably smell bad, too. Oh, all right. Mike? No, he's not here. I don't know where he is. You know how cameramen are; he wandered off to find something to eat and I haven't seen him since. I don't know how he can stand to eat anything here. The whole place turns my stomach. All right, yeah, all right, live at five. *(Back to the other conversation.)* You won't believe this. You simply will not believe this. Now they want me to stay here all afternoon and do a live shot at five. Some puff piece on one of these kids and their smelly animals. How am I ever going to make it to a major market if my portfolio is cute kid stories? You remember Meredith, from college? The blonde? Well, she was a bottle blonde, but still... Her first station they put her on the consumer affairs beat and she like got to go out and ambush unscrupulous tattoo artists who were using second-rate inks that caused their tattoos to fade, that sort of thing. Legitimate scandals. One guy got this tattoo that said "I love Freda," but the last letter faded, so it just said "I love Fred." Now she's like the substitute weekend anchor and is starting to get feelers from major markets. But no, not me, I've got the county fair assignment! Oh, OK, well, I guess I should go too. I'll talk to you later, OK? Bye bye, snugglebunny. I love you, too. Smoochies! *(Hangs up the phone; looks around for her cameraman.)* Mike! Mike! Where did that lazy creep go? Mike! Mike!

THE KATRINA PROJECT:
HELL AND HIGH WATER

Michael Marks and Mackenzie Westmoreland

Jackie Bolton denounces the government's spin on Hurricane Katrina and the New Orleans catastrophe.

JACKIE BOLTON. Didn't know they were there? Does he know there are 17,000 people in the Superdome? Does he know that the bathrooms are already overflowing and you can smell it all the way to Rampart Street? Does he know there is no air conditioning and old people are dying of heat exhaustion? I'm tired y'all. How can the director of FEMA not know there were people evacuating to the New Orleans Convention Center? How can we be left alone for three days with no food, no water and no help? And Barbara Bush got the nerve to tell me I'm better off than I was in my house in the ninth ward. How could they let that Amtrak train be sent from here empty with all these poor people needing a ride? How come the school buses weren't used to help us get out? Where is the President? When the hurricane hit Florida, Bush was down there two days early handing out ice personally. So what's different now? You done took all the country's money to fight a war half way round the world. Isn't it funny that all those children that we're protecting in Iraq get three meals a day and all the water they need. No wonder other countries look at us like we crazy. You treat them better than you do us. It's a war zone right here. Where's my three meals a day, Dub-yah, and all the water I need? You spend all our country's money on your homeland obscurity and can't rescue people right here at home. Maybe if Bin Laden had attacked us maybe then you'd a showed up.

KID-SIMPLE: A RADIO PLAY IN THE FLESH

Jordan Harrison

Moll, 16, addresses Garth, 16, who has just broken her heart and stolen her greatest invention ever. Garth, it turns out, is really a sinister shapeshifter called The Mercenary.

MOLL. I will get you for this, Garth. The world will have to go without new inventions for some time, because all my ingenuity will be directed toward your undoing. I will get you for messing with my machine and my sanity. All of CREATION will get you. You will be FOOD. A plane will drop you over the unforgiving Serengeti with a faulty parachute, an empty canteen, no sunblock— and when one of these circumstances fells you, you will finally do some good on this planet as recycled material. Your meat will invigorate the ecosystem,
your stumpy remains will feed the beasties of the earth:

Lions and tigers and nuclear apes.
Crocs and bears and mean, mean dogs!

Unprotected from the African sun, your eyes will shrivel into tiny raisins—the albino kind no one favors—and you will be alone, totally alone, for so long that proximity to another body is *novel*. And when you think you'll never see a human face again, I'll swoop in, *deus ex machina*, to say simply: 'Sup.

Your stumpy remains are so glad to see me, looking up to me like a god. But instead of kisses or cool clear water I serve you up a subpoena, bringing to the fore your crimes against United States patent law!

MAY ALL THIS COME TO PASS. The loneliness most of all.

LANGUAGE OF ANGELS

Naomi Iizuka

Kendra remembers the night Celie vanished in a cave.

KENDRA. It was dark that night, it was so dark. There was some candles we brought along, to make it all spooky like, shadow light, fire light, but once you got beyond the opening, once you got inside, there wasn't no light. Celie was talking out loud. I remember it was funny to me, what she said. I thought it was the funniest thing in the world. I forget what it was, what she was saying.
It could've been some tiny thing—
It could've been nothing at all—
After that, I don't know. I forget. I try to put this all behind me. I'm not the same person I was then. I don't even hardly know who that girl was anymore.
Celie was—
She was nice.
She was different, touched, like she got the shine, you know, like she was seeing things different, seeing things we don't see. In her room, she used to have tacked up on the wall pictures of angels, beautiful boys with muscles and all, and they're all bare chested with their big strong arms and chests—only thing different being the wings. Beautiful boys with wings. I didn't get all that when I was little, all that stuff about angels and god in heaven. I thought it was all puffy clouds and angel babies playing harps. I didn't get the other part, the secret part, like some kinda sign. The language of angels, and how light burns.

LARK

Romulus Linney

Thea, a sixteen-year-old piano prodigy, feels slighted by the chairperson of her school's Christmas show when her rival has been shown special preference. She tells her brother Thor what has happened.

(THEA *goes to one side of the stage and takes up* THOR, *now a bigger puppet, three years older. She carries him against her hip to the center of the stage, sets him down facing her, and sits before him.*)

THEA. Here, Thor. This is an old alarm clock. It can't keep time because it's rusted out, see? But you can punch it and push the hands and sometimes it will still ding once or twice. You're the only one I can talk about this to!

(*Puppet* THOR *seems to be fooling with the old clock.*)

Thor, I hate Maisie Fischer! I want to kill her! I want to stick her on a spit and roast her over a blazing fire! I want to watch her toes shrivel up and her eyes pop out! Oh, THOR!!

(*A ding! from* THOR, *playing with the clock.*)

I didn't care about that Christmas show at school! But the entertainment committee, that means Mrs. Livery Johnson, who loves Maisie and her mother's church and hates me and my mother's church, she put Maisie Fischer down to sing, and I was down for "instrumental"!

(*A noise of clock springs from* THOR.)

All right, but I couldn't play Schubert or anything else I studied with Professor Wunsch. I had to play that boring "Western Sunsets" somebody dumb wrote for the public schools. Well, I spoke up for myself and said to Mrs. Livery Johnson this wasn't fair. She didn't like that and said, yes, she understood I was Maisie's rival in the entertainment business. So I would play "Western Sunsets" and Maisie Fischer would recite something and neither of us would sing.

(THOR *breaks something inside the clock.*)

That made me the skunk in the barn all right. Being a bad sport, which she all but said out loud to everybody. After I played that awful "Western Sunsets," badly, because I hated it, you know what Maisie Fischer did? She recited the words to "Rock of Ages"! Everybody cried, and then! then! Mrs. Livery Johnson sat down at the piano and played "Rock of Ages"! so Maisie Fischer ON DE-MAND could sing it! Everybody stood up and clapped and cheered and Maisie Fischer stood there smirking at me and everybody knew why! I couldn't play Schubert or sing anything. I made a hundred and fifty new enemies all at once! School! School!!

(*The alarm in the old clock rings.*)

You got that thing to ring? Well, SHUT IT OFF! *(In tears,* THEA *takes the clock from* THOR *and shuts the alarm off.)* I know I'm awful, and shouldn't be like this. But I can't help it! And this time, I don't care!

(THOR *cries.* THEA *picks him up and sets him against her hip again.*)

Hush, Thor. I didn't mean to upset you. Hush, let's go home. What's next, Thor? That's what I want to know. What's next?

LUNA PARK

Caridad Svich

Monica describes what it was like to go for an amusement park record on the Shock Drop ride on a semi-enchanted day one summer, a day that was marked by public tragedy.

MONICA. I was going for the record that day.
Nobody'd done the Shock Drop more than ten times.
Certainly not in Luna Park, anyway.
At first it was just routine. I just wanted the thrill of testing myself
The way I always did. But then I got fierce about it. Like Lance Armstrong or something.
I didn't even care if I got sick. I would wear my sickness with pride.
I took over the ride.
The guy running it knew I was on a quest.
Like when my cousin Marcy took over karaoke night at the Vinyl Lounge
And belted out every song in the song bible until she got through every one.
Or like when that artist said she wanted to film Ricky Martin sleeping
Every night for twelve nights,
and then exhibit the video on a huge plasma screen across from city hall
like a shared ritualized something or other…
Can you imagine twelve nights of staring at Ricky Martin in deep REM?
I mean, I'm not into him, but if I was…

Anyway, I was on the Shock Drop on my little quest,
And I didn't even know why.
It was like "Today I will kick some Shock Drop ass."
It wasn't logical. I didn't plan it out. I just went on impulse.

I do things like that. You can ask Leslie or Kayla. They know. I just go.
And the guy running the ride was really cool.
He respected my quest.
Cause he understood on some spiritual, earth-baby level
That some things are meant to be done.

At first I got sick. And I don't usually get sick
Cause I've got major stamina,
and then it was like I was on some supernatural high.
My body was in this ride,
Being plunged from zero to fifty, and I couldn't even feel it.
I didn't get dizzy or freaked out.
I was above things somehow. Everybody in the park was this gigantic blur,
And I was pure adrenaline like those drinks at the nutritional store:
Ripped fuel. That was me.

And then everything stopped. Just like that.
The blur crystallized,
And all I could think about was what Ricky Martin would look like sleeping.

Luna Park

Caridad Svich

Leslie looks back on a summer day filled with beauty, boys, soccer, falling in love in an instant, a day of public tragedy, and coming together.

LESLIE. I don't always look at the boys. But they were having so much fun
And they were…yummy. So, why not look?
Some were in their rock n' roll T-shirts.
Others were in little raggedy shorts and no tops.
Really buff in a non muscle-man kind of way.
Others were in soccer clothes. You could tell they played on a team somewhere.
They spoke a different language. I could make out bits of words. Latin-sounding.
One of them told me about Luna Park—another one in some other country—
Where the best musicians play. "Like Madison Square Garden." he said.
Another one told me about a park just like this one, only bigger,
Where families come and spend their weekends.
They all talked about the sun, and time.
Letting time pass, and how in this park named after a moon—luna, luna, luna—
they felt protected by the sun.

After the match, the boys in the rock n'roll shirts headed for drinks by the stand.
Kayla and Lee met up.
She's sweet on him. I don't know why.
But I waved them on, anyway, cause I'm her friend.
The unfamiliar boys wanted to explore the park. I went along with them.

Most of them came from nervous towns. They knew all about fear,
How it gets into you, and how it's a very real thing and not just,
you know,
Something somebody talks about scientifically on the TV.
They said they lived with dynamite in their lives,
Daily explosions,
And so they lived with the knowledge
that something awful could happen at any moment…
But also how something good can happen too,
And how beautiful that was—
I couldn't make out all their words, but I listened anyway.

Soon we were at the cliffs. Right below.
The sun was beaming something unreal.
They were bands of boys and girls diving, and others by the pool,
making noise.
It was a glorious day. I wanted to scream. In a good way.
But I didn't. I just let one of the boys kiss me.
He was all sweaty from the soccer, and his clothes were sticky.
He spoke his language. He told me things. He had history in his
eyes.
I touched his chest. He was so strong. But fragile too. He didn't
hide from me.
I told him we could sit by the deep end of the pool, splash around
if we wanted.
He told me the pool-water smelt like violets,
and we could pretend like we were in an ancient place.

I looked up. Flaco and Cory were about to dive. They were a pic-
ture.
Their legs in position, their arms outstretched.
"How beautiful," I said.
My boy whispered something in my ear.
I leaned close.
When I looked back up, no one was in sight.

MEMORY HOUSE

Kathleen Tolan

Katia is a wry and strong-willed high school senior who was adopted from Russia at a young age. She struggles to write an essay for her college application.

KATIA. Well what do I write? That I'm a victim from a bleeding country?

That I owe my life to the people who took advantage of the tragedy of Russia and ripped me off which was great cuz now I don't have to be a hooker on the streets of Moscow but—oops—now I'm a citizen of the country of bullies?

And all these other countries and people hate us because we're bombing them and fucking with them and I'm the spoils of that. I don't know where to go, what to do—go back to Russia? Why would I do that? Stay here? Why would I do that?

　(Beat.)

Meanwhile my friends are all totally freaking out about their fucking stupid test scores and their totally inane application essays and jackass interviews and their parents are all flipping out and acting like their kids are trying to kill them, as if their kids are thinking about them at all, this is so totally not about them and they think it is and so they have to deal with debilitating lunatic parents on top of everything else.

　(Beat.)

And I'm thinking, don't they get that we're the bad guys? And don't look at me like this is some teenage thing or some psychological thing or like you have to protect me and go along. There are people getting killed, people dying, this fine country that saved me from a terrible life is sending soldiers to poor countries to kill innocent people. And you know what? If I were tending my blueberries, just trying to eke out some way to feed my children and live with the simplicity and the joy and the hardship of the sun in the morning and the moon at night, and just getting the blueberry on the truck for the man with the clogged arteries to drive it up to you for your pie, just doing my back-breaking work, and doing my best, and out of the big sky came a bomb that tore up my field and killed my dear children and my dear wife and my dear friends and neighbors and I had *nothing* and it was because this big rich country wanted to get some guys they thought might be hiding somewhere who were lunatics or who were so angry and no one was helping them and they were so fucking angry that they had strapped a bomb to their backs and they were willing to explode their lives, to just blow them up because they were so insane and angry and desperate. How would I feel? What would be the thing to do?

MISS KENTUCKY

Allison Williams

Shayleen, a teenage beauty pageant contestant, is inadvertently locked out of the convention center after stepping outside for a cigarette. In the alley out back, Shayleen implores her mother to understand that she just wants to be a normal girl.

SHAYLEEN. Just as pretty when we're comin' out of the shower with our hair in a cap, but not like this. They put on those dresses and those banners and their helpers and their tape and shine up their teeth just like me, but there's somethin' else they're putting on. Somethin' hard. I don't mean they're mean, exactly, 'cause they're all real friendly and nice, and they really mean it, but they're meaning it as hard as they can. It's like this force field of nice-ness that's stickin' out about three feet from their body.

(Pause.)

I guess that sounds pretty silly.

I was back there in the wings, and all those force fields were all around me, bashin' into each other, crowdin' me out, and I had to get away or I was just going to scream, and I came out here, and I realized, this was the first time I have breathed like a normal person in years. The first time I'm not busy being all nice to everyone to keep the reputation of the title. I mean—have I been carryin' around one of those force fields with me?

Sittin' on that bucket, I realized I'm about sick of underprivileged children and shut-in seniors and autism awareness. I want...I want to go to the mall. And I wanna buy a pair of washed-out denim jeans and a t-shirt without a collar and I wanna wear red nylon underwear.

Okay, maybe not that part. But don't you see, Mama? I want to be selfish!

A MOST CURIOUS PHENOMENON
(full-length version)

Alan Haehnel

Dixie epitomizes the misunderstood, infatuated teenager.

DIXIE. What do you mean I can't go out with Johny tonight? Why not? *(She listens, as if to a parent.)* I've been spending too much time with him? Are you crazy? I haven't been spending enough time with him! Don't you understand that I love him? You don't even know what love is! I know what you think; you think this is just some little fling. Puppy love. An infatuation! That's what I heard you tell Mrs. Ricker at the grocery store. You're always talking about me behind my back, but I know! I know! You can't keep me away from Johny! He's the only thing that matters to me in my whole life! I'll run away! I'll…I'll kill myself! I will! If you don't let me see him, I'll jump off a bridge! You think I'm kidding, but I am not! My life isn't worth living without Johny! *(Listening for a moment.)* Don't tell me you understand; don't even try to tell me that. If you understood, you wouldn't try to keep my away from the one true thing in my life, the one true love of my life. Me and Johny were meant to be together. We have to be together! Don't you understand that I need him? Don't you understand that he is all I need to survive? I don't need to do my homework or clean my room or "uphold my family obligations"—all this crap you've been telling me. I need my Johny! I don't even need to eat or drink or sleep! I just need Johny! I need him! I need him! You don't understand me one…tiny…bit!

A MOST CURIOUS PHENOMENON
(full-length version)

Alan Haehnel

Myriam is six years old. She fidgets her way through this school report about Valentine's Day.

MYRIAM. For my holiday report I'm going to do a report about Valentine's Day. I have a poster here that I made. Um, I made all the hearts and my mom wrote some of the words because I couldn't get them to be big and still fit on the poster. Anyway, um, Valentine's Day wasn't always a holiday. Before it was a holiday it was just February 14th, which is sometimes on a Monday and sometimes on another day like Wednesday. And sometimes it's on a Thursday, but it's not always on a Thursday like Thanksgiving. And it doesn't have turkeys, either. Um, Valentine's Day is named after a man named Valentine. *(Reading from her notes:)* He was a priest back when everybody was a Roman, and he married people even when a general said that they couldn't be married because then they would be too busy being married to go and fight in wars. Valentine got in trouble and got his head cut off. And died. And so, a few years later, in 496 A.D., the Emperor Gela…Gelatine said that, from then on, everybody had to have Valentine's Day on February 14th to celebrate when St. Valentine got his head chopped off. And so now, we send cards and make cards and we have candy for Valentine's. My mother usually gets all of us kids a big box of candy that we're supposed to share. And that's how we're supposed to show our love on Valentine's, by sharing, except my little brother doesn't like nuts so he bites into the chocolates to see if they have nuts and if they do he just puts them back in the box with teeth marks on them and I hate that so I usually hit him which I probably shouldn't do on Valentine's Day. But it's my favorite holiday because I love the colors pink and red and I love getting candy.

The End. *(She pauses, as if getting a question from the teacher.)* What does A.D. stand for? Um…I think it's…after dinner?

MULLEN'S ALLEY

Timothy Mason

Rebeccah, a poor Jewish girl, exults over her new glasses and restored sight.

REBECCAH. Yes, he gave them to me! Terry Dolan! He took me to the Children's Aid Society and a man there put so very many glasses on my face and then, all of a sudden, I could see—I can see, Lily! And the charge was two dollars and Terry Dolan paid it right then and there! I've been all over, looking. You know the great tree on Mott Street, near the church?

I've been living my life seeing only a blur of green. But thousands and thousands of leaves, each leaf sharp and clear and different from every other? This I did not know! And grass is not a carpet painted one color only, grass is blades, there in St. Patrick's church-yard, among the graves, millions of little green soldiers, waving at me, Hello, klein Beccah! Lily, I taught myself to read with the books this close to my face, but now I can walk along the Mulberry Bend and read the signs from where I stand, thousands of words, everywhere I look!

> (REBECCAH *moves off, looking at all she can see, reading the signs as she leaves*)

"Dutch's Dry Goods." "Hammerstein's Stables." "Rosen's Diner." "Klein and Company, Knickerbockers," I never was so proud!

OVER THE TAVERN

Tom Dudzick

The year is 1959. Annie Pazinski, 16, makes a midnight confession to her mother. It concerns a rumor going around that some girl in the neighborhood was seen undressing in front of her window at night, with the shade up, on purpose!

ANNIE. *(Upset.)* Okay, here's what happened. The other day, me and Tina, we sort of took a long lunch hour at school. How long? Oh…about the length of a movie. Tina said that these two boys would meet us at the theatre. From Bishop Cleary. They take long lunch hours, too, sometimes. It didn't seem like a great idea, but since boys haven't exactly been beating down my door. Anyway, they never showed up. They got caught by the school janitor. So, me and Tina went in. And, this movie, it was sort of artistic. Foreign, actually. I don't think it was on the Legion of Decency list. But it wasn't one of those dirty movies! Oh, no, it was beautiful. It really was! And so romantic, I just wanted to die! It took place in this little town in Italy. And there was this one part where this girl's father forbids her to see her lover and he locks her in her room. So, that night, while her lover is outside, she goes to her window and, sort of. gets ready for bed. …But they didn't show anything! They covered most of it with trees and stuff and showing his face looking up at her. It was so artistic! And, so anyway, all day I couldn't stop thinking about that part. And that night I couldn't sleep 'cause all I could think about was how she loved him so. And him outside all alone. And then, lying there in bed, thinking, I just sort of became the girl. I got up out of bed, and. Oh, Mama, I never thought anybody would be watching. I swear! *(Sobs.)*

THE REALM

Sarah Myers

Laura stands alone in the open air. This is a future not too far from now. She speaks to a son who isn't there to hear her words, one she was forced to abandon.

LAURA. Back when there were actually days of the week, I used to watch egg sacs outside my window with specks of waiting spiders inside. When they hatched, they stuck to each other in their little cotton web and waved their arms in the air. Like tentacles. There's a better word for that. Tentacles. I just don't know it anymore. I was only able to hold on to half my Language, so I leave what's left in the air, in your ears, offered up and around and ahead and because when you see what you see what my life used to be used to see used to be like. Before.

The spiders left empty cotton globes of air, stuck between the pane and the screened-in sky outside. There was sky outside then. There was a thing called inside, and we lived in it, and then we went outside. And there were windows with glass panes. Not plastic. And no real notion of life lived underground. So now I dream of days of the week. Just days of the week. A real week. And trees. Traffic. Sandwiches. Simple things that need no explanation. Someone singing nursery rhymes.

(She hums the opening bars of "The Itsy Bitsy Spider.")

There was a song I sang when you were young. I can't remember the words, but I remember when I started to forget them. It was back when we discovered that everything was as easy to lose as daylight. After the seven-day week ended and the fourteen-day week began, we waited for a new era when there might be children who ate sandwiches and sang. But by the time the days of the week ended altogether, we only wished we'd never wanted water.

THE ROOM FULL OF ANNIE

Annika Rosenvinge

Annie, confined in a mental asylum, remembers her boyfriend Tom as a first-grade boy.

ANNIE. *(Watches him go, then turns to panel:)* He never really said all that. It never happened. It could have though, because I imagined it. I read once that anything imaginable is feasible. One of the best things I ever read. Tom could have said those things. Maybe he would have, eventually. Or maybe I'm lying to myself. Sometimes it's so difficult to distinguish between lies and what's sensible. I have trouble. Just like my mama. *(Laughs softly, looks around her.)* Earliest memory I have of Tom. This retard in our first-grade class shit his pants, and he was rubbing it on his fingers, crying. Even the teacher wouldn't go near him, just herded us away like he was dangerous or rabid. Tom took him to the sink, showed him to wash up. Retard loved Tom after that, followed him around, brought him stuff. Tom never said anything mean, just listened to him babbling and said gravely "That's interesting, Clancy, thank you for telling me." Jesus. *(Cries.)* Why the hell is he so good? I want to hate him for something, but Tom's so good. Looks after the fucking retards, me and Clancy. *(Pause.)* Clancy, incidentally, electrocuted himself with a toaster. Poking a knife where he shouldn't. He was a retard. Tom, though, sometimes I disbelieve that he exists. He slips out of my mind like flies through a rabbit trap. Tom? Tom? Hey, why don't you guys ever talk? Please? *(Addresses the panel:)* Sometimes I think that this will all just end, you know, like some day you guys will write up a little report cautioning me to take my vitamins, but hey, I'm free to go. Free, safe, and sound! Healthy, happy, chipper as can be! But then I look at you and I know—I won't ever be pure enough. I'm a natural red-blooded gal! I got to sashay the streets while I'm in my prime. I've seen you lookin' Brown Eyes!

Maybe you and me could have a little party. Wouldn't be much talking, we could do it private like—without all your friends here. What do you say, sweetheart? *(Laughs without humor.)* Just foolin'.

SCHOOLGIRL FIGURE

Wendy MacLeod

Renee, now Queen of The Carpenters, lies dying of anorexia in a hospital bed. Abandoned by her rightful consort The Bradley and her best friend Patty, who has decided to eat normally, Renee tries to convince the audience of the need for perfection.

RENEE. No great loss. Patty will be happier in the Midwest—parkas camouflage a multitude of sins. And as for The Bradley, he wasn't really the prize, he was just the tacky little statuette; the gas station glasses, the stuffed bear at the fair! The prize is actually…well, true story. Back in the days when I had muscles, I would rent a patch of ice every morning before it was light and go out there and try to master my school figures. I would fiercely skate that figure eight, because down the pike the school figures would count for 50% of my Olympic score. I practiced them even when I was on land, waiting in line for the water fountain, pressing my sneakers into imaginary blades. I spent the wee hours of my pre-pubescence obsessed with the Russian judge's good opinion of my outside edge and do you know what happened? They did away with the school figure part of the competition. Just did away with it. Because nobody saw them. Nobody <u>wanted</u> to see them. The audience just cared about the part where a skinny girl wears a skimpy leotard trimmed with maribou and jumps around to a disco version of Carmen. What can we learn from this? I'm sorry…I forgot what I was going to say. Is it cold in here or is it just me? Oh, I know. What we have learned is that there is only so much in this world that we can control so by all means let us control what we can, achieve what we must. Perfection.

> *(When she speaks in rhyme we realize she's imagining herself in The Pantheon of dead girls.)*

If you're happy with who you are
It's clearly time to raise the bar
Now it's time for my good-byeses
To you poor girls of the larger sizes

> *(A triumphant* RENEE *looks at the audience pityingly as she gets on the gurney. The gurney taxis her out.)*

Science Fair

Jeanmarie Williams

Michelle, 15, an earnest girl scout, presents her science fair project to a panel of judges. She is a strange breather, and perhaps this is why she is the way she is—a loner, a strange walker, strange voice, a little wrecked around the edges combined with a mean dignity that holds her up.

MICHELLE. Hypothesis. Girl Scout Cookies, the Great Leveler. Also. There's people living all around you that you don't even know the first thing about. Also. Looking at how we all respond to Girl Scout cookie season can show that we are all the same inside. Even if we're not all the same outside. Not because anyone else is better on the outside than other people, because that's not true.

I have a calling, as you can see from the way I take pride in my uniform from Girl Scout Troop Number 567. I use starch and so on. The other girls don't use starch but that's because I'm the oldest scout and I need to set a good example.

Methodology. Walking versus riding.

To sell cookies, sure, you can walk around the neighborhood. And the girls who walk around the neighborhood have the spirit of Girl Scout cookies in their hearts, I don't doubt that and so on, but of course everyone there is going to buy cookies; they've done it for years as their parents have done for years and so on all the way back to the first cookie drive.

This is called "selling the cookies to the people who already know they want them."

You can also find the people who need the cookies. I get on my horse every day after school and travel across the fields of my neighbors and I visit with them, that's what you have to do out here. Sometimes they invite me inside. And then they have to buy cookies because I've traveled all that way on horseback just to bring them their Thin Mints and Do-Si-Does and so on. So what I do is sell cookies so that my troop can go camping in the summer and all that, but I'm also fulfilling a service requirement. I should get a merit badge for all this and all those people in my troop know it.

And this is called "selling the cookies to the people who might not otherwise get them."

Then there's the Indians.

Selling Girl Scout cookies to Indians is no easy thing to do. First you have to get yourself in the mind of what it was like when they were happy, because you're selling a happy thing and you want to come at them like you're happy, too, in the way they used to be happy.

So I ride my horse a little farther out. Because there's all these people out there with no shot of any cookies at all. And to get to them, you have to ride a horse because my father won't drive me to the reservation because the roads are bad for his car and so on.

At first, to get happy, I taught myself to yodel.

(She demonstrates.)

I didn't know any Indian songs. And then I started to make up poems about the people on the gravestones on the reservation and so on. And that made me happy and also made me think about how their culture was ruined and this made me feel the things that they feel.

And it also made me think about how everybody dies, how things happen to us, like people die and so on, and it doesn't matter what color you are, because your family is still dead. And riding my horse, that makes me happy like Indians must have been happy.

When all the cookies are in, and that's usually when it's pretty cold around here, I get on my horse and deliver all the cookies to all the farmers and those people on the Indian Reservation, but they don't buy much because they're poor and all that. But that's okay. Girl Scout cookies make people really happy and the way I figure, that's what I do, I make people happy. And my parents have taught me that you should always figure out what poor people need and then you should give it to them whether they ask for it or not.

And this is called "selling the cookies to the people who didn't know they wanted them."

What my research found out is that the people on the reservation always choose the cookies that are colorful and have happier designs. It's just like the clothes they wear for special days and so on. They don't go in for Thin Mints as much as the Do-Si-Does and other cookies with stripes and different colors all on the same cookie.

Interpretation.

Art is everywhere around here. And you only have to try your best to be happy so that you can see it. And you shouldn't think about the people who make you too sad, but you should put all of that away so you can use it later.

Because did you know that I would tell my poems to the Indians and that they would laugh, but it was a good laugh. At first they wouldn't talk to me, they closed their doors and so on. I must have looked very official in my uniform and maybe that made them scared of me.

Also they taught me how to dance because one of the girls is my friend now and she invites me to places that only Indians are allowed to go.

I think that, oh— Conclusion.

I think that the Indians are superior to white people. They are friendlier and have more dances that mean something and they always buy the cookies that are more beautiful and more delicious and so on.

Also it's important to figure out what people need, and then you should give it to them because that makes us all the same. The way Girl Scout cookies are all the same. Every Samoan looks the same as another Samoan.

And I can dance like anybody else on the reservation.

(MICHELLE *dances as the lights fade.*)

THE SEQUENCE

Vincent Delaney

In a not so distant future, where DNA determines everything from education to choice of friends, Jasmine shares the nightmare of discovering what it means to be an outsider.

JASMINE. I went back. All the way home. Walked for two weeks, you know that? You think I could walk two weeks straight, out here, no food, no water, in this weather? I did though. That way. Like I knew which way to go: that way. At night there's stars. Not the holograms, not phony, but real. So cold and bright they hurt your heart, just to look at. Maybe you find water, a stream, not controlled, just goes wherever it feels like going. Maybe there's stuff to eat, if you're not particular. I talked the whole first day. Thought I was talking to myself, keep brave: what's new, how you feeling, how's the day going? Figured out I was talking to my mom. That she was calling me home. I made it. Starved, scared, thirsty, but I found it, my place. Hid outside by the main lock, waited til dark, found a way in. No one was going to stop me, not now. I would have fought a bear at this point. Maybe I did, I was pretty worked up, I might have fought a bear and forgot all about it. Went to my house. Wiped my face, I was a little dirty, I wanted to look good. For when they would hug me. For when they would cry. For my sister, and my little brother, just a baby. For my dad. My mom. Maybe I smelled a little ripe, who wouldn't, fourteen days in the outside? Opened the door. Stepped inside. They were eating. At the table. Mom, dad, sister, brother. They looked up. Stared at me. Not a word. Sure, they knew it was me. Nobody moved. Something turned in my stomach. All kinds of bells went off in my stomach. Mom starts to cry. Sob, sob, sob. Won't look at me. Sister takes my brother upstairs. My dad gets up. Just stares at me. Like a mask, just

stares, no expression. That's when I knew: you can't go back. This is our home now.

SHUN THE HEAVEN

Alan Haehnel

Hoping for a large payoff, Ruth risks the lives of her clairvoyant but disabled twin sisters. Here, she rebuts her mother's argument that Ruth should consider the consequences of her actions for the next world.

RUTH. This world is all I know, Mamma! I don't see your next world! I don't see your God! In this world, we are poor and other people are rich! In this world, Mamma, we drive a piece of crap car and other people drive a Mercedes Benz. In this world, I bring them their food and they throw away half of it and I'm hungry! In this world, Mamma, I am always, always hungry! This world is what I know. This world! This world is where Frank is and where I am and where we're going to get married and try to build something better. You've got everything here to keep yourself happy, Mamma. You've got the twins; you've got their miracles; you've even got a Reverend who will come over and lay his hands on you whenever you want. You've got yourself a crummy piece of heaven here already, but guess what? I don't have nothing. Not a thing in this world. And I want something. And I'm going to get it.

SPRING

Tanya Palmer

Wendy, a popular high school senior, defends her desire to help people in need.

WENDY. I can help. I just think, look, God gave me everything a girl could ever hope for. A loving family, a beautiful house, a new car, I do well in school, and I don't mean to sound conceited or anything, but gosh, just about everybody likes me. And sometimes I look at other people in our school, like that girl in our math class with the terrible rash all over her face, or those girls who hang out by the corner store smoking and looking mean and you just know they're going to end up pregnant and on welfare. I just want to, I don't know, pick them up and hold them to me, or I don't know, swallow up some of their pain. Because that's one thing I just don't have, that kind of pain, waking up everyday knowing that people are going to stare and turn away, or someone's going to tell you you're stupid, or you have to be lifted into your wheelchair…the other night I dreamt that I was paralyzed from the waist down and my arms didn't work anyway cause they were these little flippers, not really arms at all, and half my face kinda hung down and I was drooling and there was a room full of people staring and laughing and turning away in disgust, and I woke up feeling, peaceful almost. Happy.

SPRING

Tanya Palmer

Ilsa has just been asked by the popular girl in class to explain the scars on her arms. Not looking for a shoulder to cry on, Ilsa rejects this offer of friendship, refusing to let the situation turn into another pop culture cliché.

ILSA. Yeah right. Listen, Wendy, that's your name right? I know what this is about. You come out here thinking, you're going to help the poor freaky girl with all her pain, you know, share in her suffering. She'll open up to you cause you've been there too. Sure it doesn't look like you have a clue about anything but hanging out at the mall, but you've felt the pain, and you're here to tell me, it's going to be all right. I'll cry on your shoulder and then you'll take me into the bathroom and put some lipstick on me and a ribbon in my hair like Molly Ringwald and Ally Sheedy in The Breakfast Club, then we'll be friends and you'll invite me to your parties, and I'll get a really cute boyfriend, like one of those guys on the football team, and then I'll be so happy and fulfilled I won't have to slice myself up anymore, and I'll have you to thank for it. Well, let me tell you, that's not how it's going to work. First of all, I cut myself cause I like it. I like the way it feels. And I already have a boyfriend and plenty of parties to go to, so why don't you go back to the other side and eat your celery sticks and talk about what you're going to wear to the prom.

VIEWS

Mrinalini Kamath

David and Diane were high school sweethearts who married after Diane became pregnant with their now two-year-old son Billy. When David comes home one day, announcing that he's quit his job, Diane suddenly realizes that she and David are not on the same page about their marriage.

DIANE. What was I supposed to do, tell you what you wanted to hear so you could go off to Georgetown and play basketball? Well, I'm sorry David, but for some crazy reason, I felt I had to tell you the truth, and that is exactly what I told you. I could never have had an abortion. If I ever had any doubts about it before, now that Billy's here, I *know* I could never go through with it. And my parents would've kicked me out. I told you the facts. If you married me because you felt guilty, that is *your* fault, not mine. I didn't force you to have sex with me, and I certainly didn't put a gun to your head telling you to propose to me. *(Pause.)* You know, *I* would've liked to have gone to college. Maybe I didn't get a scholarship to some hot-shot university, but I could've gone to college, could've made friends, could've had *fun*. But I made my choice, and now I have to live with it. You made yours.

WAVING GOODBYE

Jamie Pachino

Lily Blue is a 17-year-old photographer who recently lost her father in a mountain climbing accident, and must spend her 17th year with the mother who abandoned her. Here, Lily speaks about seeing her mother's artwork for the first time. (Note: Lily and her mother have just had an argument, during which they accidentally shattered one of Amanda's pieces of sculpture. The line "This was my favorite thing she ever did" refers to the broken art in front of her).

LILY. Boggy sometimes I dream my father falls, and I can catch him. I race and I grope until I'm standing right under him, with my arms open wide. But instead his weight crushes me, and nobody survives. Sometimes my father dies because I'm too insignificant to break his fall. *(Enormously hurt:)* This was my favorite thing she ever did. I was ten when I saw it the first time. She had gone off to…the Serengeti I think. The month of March is supposed to be, I don't know—she has this thing about light and water and—she'd gone off before, but this time we were pretty sure she wasn't coming back. And he had to go off on a climb. The hot water heater was busted, the mortgage was overdue—again, Pepper our dog— needed an operation, and he had to leave. So he took me to this locker where she kept her early stuff, because he wanted me to know something about her. To understand why she was right, he said, to go away when the world asked her to, because of what the world got back. Not me, not him, just…the world. But there aren't so many ways to say that to a ten-year-old, so he took me to see her work. I didn't know anything about Art, but something about the forearms and the hands…my father's hands that she had done…

He showed me all the work she'd done right after they met, and told me how she ate Hershey bars at 12,000 feet after climbing without any of the right equipment, and how it was a miracle she didn't die right there. He smiled so big when he explained how those first pieces made her name, how her vision of him had made her—who she turned into—even though she had grown past them and wouldn't look at them anymore. Even though they were his favorites, and my favorites, she had to go off hunting new light. They were so incredible, I almost forgave her.

YOUNG JANE EYRE

adapted by Marisha Chamberlain
from the novel by Charlotte Bronte

Victorian era Yorkshire. Jane Eyre, age 10, reflects to herself how to survive at the orphanage known as Lowood School.

JANE EYRE. This was not the kind of schooling I imagined—no stacks of books to read, no globes, no maps; but rather, an endless repetition of little facts that no one seemed to care about. I didn't care, either, that two times two was four and Rome, the capital of Italy. Breakfast would soon be over and yet no one was eating. I wondered how these girls kept alive—for it was apparent that this was not the first time breakfast had been spoiled. I thought they must survive like the bushes and trees, taking their nourishment from the ground they stood upon. As for me, I knew I must eat, and if I must learn to eat burned porridge, then I would gnash it down.

Nine o'clock was geography and history; ten, grammar; ten-thirty, penmanship, and eleven to twelve, an entire hour of arithmetic. Punished for a splotch on her dress, Helen Burns stood calmly the whole time with the sign round her neck saying in French that she was a pig. Had it been I, I should have wanted the earth to open up and swallow me whole. But she—she seemed lost in a daydream. I'd seen in her eyes that she was far away—in some other country or on some distant star.

I should be delighted to be good if I knew what that was. We were to obey dozens of rules and all of them unwritten. I was to keep my mouth shut. I was to watch out—to expect cruelty and hardness. And now, what was I to make of sudden kindness Helen showed to me? What kind of place was this? What was I to say when suddenly asked to speak up and not to be afraid?

I told Helen this: If people are always kind and obedient to those who are cruel and unjust, the wicked people would have it all their own way. I wanted to stand with you this morning because I know what it is to be disliked for no reason. I must hate those who, whatever I do to please them, persist in hating me. I should like to strike back at such people so hard as to teach them never to strike me again. Gently she challenged me: does violence overcome hatred. I told her I'd strike with words. She wanted to know, would that make peace? If I want to make peace, I'll keep silent, but if I have principles, I'll speak up.

Male or Female

AFTER MATH

Jonathan Dorf

A student has just witnessed the disappearance of a classmate in the middle of math class. Where are the dark-suited man and woman taking Emmett, and why is the teacher shaking?

SHAKING STUDENT. Mrs. Parks has this thing about tests. Well, she has this thing about everything, but when it comes to tests… If she's giving a test, you don't knock on the door, you don't stand by the door, you don't call the room, you don't even look in the window. And not just the students—the other teachers, even Mr. Bobell, the principal.

(Beat.)

One time, he knocks and comes in during a quiz—not even a test—a quiz on solving simple equations. You know, like x squared equals nine, or three x plus x equals eight. That's algebra. You should see how she looks at him. Her eyes get all narrow, and I'm not crazy so I know I'm not really seeing it, but I swear there's these flames shooting from her eyes. Or maybe it's lasers. I think it's flames, though, 'cause if I didn't know better, I'd say there's smoke comin' from her ears. And Mr. Bobell starts to say something, only nothing comes out. His jaw flaps in slow-mo, then flaps again. He takes one step back, two steps back—and he's gone.

(Beat.)

But today, we're in the middle of a major test—not just some quiz. This is an all-out unit test. Points, lines, slopes—we're graphing 'til we can't graph no more.

(Like a rapper:)

Graph those lines in the air—graph 'em like you just don't care.

(Beat.)

Anyway, this man in a dark gray suit walks in, and there's a woman—also wearing a dark gray suit—at the door, and I watch Mrs. Parks's eyes start to ignite, only the man doesn't flinch—and her eyes, they sink back into her head, like they're in retreat.

(Beat.)

He says something to her real quiet, and her eyes…her eyes totally wash out, and her face wipes blank. "Emmett," she says, "bring your books." And Emmett packs his books into his backpack and goes with the suits—the man inside and the woman at the door.

(Beat.)

And when the door closes and Emmett is gone and the suits are gone, it's "back to your tests. Ten minutes." But I don't believe her. Yeah, I believe we've got ten minutes of class. I can see the clock, but I don't believe Mrs. Parks cares if we finish, and as she picks up Emmett's test, her hands—I'm not crazy, so I know my head's just making it up—I swear her hands are shaking.

ANON(YMOUS)

Naomi Iizuka

Anon has fled the country where he was born. Anon dreams of his mother.

ANON.
Where I come from is far away from here.
Where I come from there was a war that lasted so long
People forgot what they were fighting for.
Where I come from bombs rained down from the sky night after night
And boys wandered the streets with M-16s.
Where I come from mines are planted in the roads like deadly flowers,
And the air smells like death, rank and sticky sweet.
Where I come from you go to sleep at night
And dream about the faces of the people you love.

You dream the face of the one person you love. And that person, that person becomes like home. Their eyes. Their skin. Their voice, the sound of their voice. And so you dream about that person. You dream about home. You dream about going home.

ATWATER: FIXIN' TO DIE

Robert Myers

Soon after the election of George H.W. Bush, an African-American student at Howard University denounces the naming of Lee Atwater, Bush's campaign manager and the architect of a racially charge presidential campaign, to Howard's Board of Trustees.

STUDENT. The issue here is respect, pure and simple. I chose to study at Howard because it represents a certain tradition of black education in this country. I'm realistic. I know that seventy percent of our operating budget comes from the Federal government, and the administration of this school has no choice but to deal with whoever's in the White House. There's been a history of white patronage of black education and institutions and artists for decades in America, everybody from Zora Neale Hurston to Tuskegee Institute, and nobody who's protesting here is against white people serving on the board of Howard per se. But I'm not going to sit idly by when the man who engineered THE most racist presidential campaign of the 20th century is named as a trustee. After these ads on TV that make "Birth of a Nation" look like "Guess Who's Coming to Dinner," he thinks he can make it all okay by serving on the board of Howard University and inviting B. B. King and a couple of other black musicians to play at the inauguration ball. He claims he wants to reach out to us and keeps emphasizing how much he loves black culture and black music and black people. It's sort of like George Wallace or Strom Thurmond saying they just love blacks, by which they mean the old shufflin' Tom who gives 'em a big smile when he serves them their lemonade on the verandah. And now Atwater tells us the whole Willie Horton thing wasn't about race. It was about crime. It was all about crime and he wishes Horton had been white. He even says if he could've been born somebody else he'd've chosen to be Bo Didley. *(Pause.)* Does anybody really believe Lee Atwater wishes he was a black man?

COMMON GROUND
Brendon Votipka

A teenager explains his current state of mind.

TEENAGER. I've been trying very hard to put into words the way I'm feeling right now. But I'm drawing a blank. I feel blank. "Blank" is almost something, but I fear it may be nothing. Nothing is an awful feeling. It's the absence of feeling. I don't feel nothing. Nothing is not what I feel. I feel something. Definitely something. I don't feel the absence of feeling, but I think I may feel the absence of color. Until I got out my art supplies from kindergarten, I couldn't decide what it was. Then, It hit me.

I feel like a white crayon. No, I don't. I am a white crayon. Exactly. I am completely and totally a white crayon. I guess I always identified with the white crayon. The thing is, the white crayon just sits in the box. You following me? I mean, I know that all the colors sit in the same box. Back in grade school, when you bought your school supplies at the beginning of a school year you could be sure that every color would be present. But while you can be sure they're all there, does it matter that every color is in the box? Does it matter if you have a white crayon? No.

The other colors get so much more action. Of course they get more action. Take a color like green. I wish I was green. Green is used in so many pictures, so often. How frequently does a kid use green. Pretty frequently. It gets a lot of action. Red is the same way. You use red for an apple, or a heart, or lips. Purple can be grapes, or flowers, or a sunset. yellow, blue, brown, black, pink, any color, you name it! People use those colors all the time. A kid uses every crayon in the box.

Except white. No one ever picks up the white crayon. It sits in its box, completely sharpened and ready to go, but it's destined to remain in the stupid box. No one needs it. It has no use. I know, I know, "people use the white crayon sometimes." But rarely. Rarely. And besides, the white crayon is the crayon no one cares if they break. If they snap it in two, no big deal. It's not like it's necessary for survival. No one needs a white crayon.

HERE AND NOW

Barry Hall

A and B, trying to figure out what went wrong in their relationship, are talking in circles. When B asks A to tell him something that is meaningful to her, A gives an anecdote about the pigeons who used to perch on the rooftops of her Catholic elementary school, which also doubles as a metaphor for their relationship.

A. You know I went to Catholic school—first grade through sixth. The church and school were built of the same gray, glittery stone—huge blocks of it. There was a bell tower—it was probably just a couple of stories high, but then it seemed… Anyway it was when I was in second grade. Pigeons used to perch on the church tower, on the church, on all the school buildings—everywhere. We used to throw rocks at them sometimes—I don't think we ever actually hit one. We were too small, and they were too far above us… Anyway, one day, the headmaster— he was also the church priest—was giving us a lecture about something—probably throwing rocks at the birds—when this huge, wet glob of pigeon shit landed right on his bald head. Splat! Of course, we all laughed. Of course, that just made Father—what was his name?—Anyway, it just made him that much angrier. I remember his face turning beet-red between streaks of white pigeon shit. From that day on, his name was Father Shithead—only when he was out of earshot, of course. But that's not the end of the story. A few days later, some workmen came and put sharp iron spikes along all the edges of the church roof, and the school, the bell tower, everywhere. They were so close together that a bird couldn't land, much less perch, or nest. The first day the pigeons kept circling, around and around, trying to land and flapping away, over and over, in total confusion. The next day, there were a few less, and the next day even less, till they had all given up. I guess they all turned Protestant. Father—

Abrams, that was his real name—told everyone it was because of some health code rule, but we all knew why. And somehow, that made him seem like even more of a shithead.

LILIES IN THE VALLEY

Gavin Lawrence

Prosecutor, boasting and vain, gives his opening arguments against a teenage couple caught dating outside their race.

PROSECUTOR. Ladies and gentlemen of the jury, citizens, distinguished guests, parents, teachers, students, fellow Americans— I'm not going to try to impress you with a bunch of legal jargon to show off my knowledge of the law. I'm not going to remind you that I graduated from Harvard University, Summa Cum Laude, at the top of my class with a double major in Biophysics and Molecular Engineering. I won't even make mention of my law degree from Georgetown University or that I was a lead dancer with Kierov Ballet in Russia. What I will say is this—these two youngsters, as innocent as they may profess to be, as harmless as they may look, are guilty, guilty, guilty. What are they guilty of you ask? Simple— they broke the law, and not just any law but the most important law to date, the most important and updated law on the books. A law that not only preserves the way of life that our ancestors fought to give us, but a law that if not defended with ferocity and diligence, could mean the end of our civilization as we know it. The end of our American way of life. The end of America—the end of us. This law which was born of the "anything goes if you associate with those" act clearly states that in this state, in this community, it is unlawful for any red blooded American citizen, born on this American soil, to knowingly and willfully engage in any kind of romantic relationship with anyone not born on American soil. It's as simple as that. The law further states that anyone convicted of breaking this law will be sent to a federal reprogramming facility for a minimum of ten years until they are deemed cured and ready for reintegration into the community. It's your job, as responsible citizens of this community to uphold this law. Your job today, is not to decide whether you like them, whether they're cute, or whether they mean well. Your job today is not to debate the law, but to uphold it. And it is my belief that once you've heard and seen the evidence, that it will be clear, without a doubt, that these two young people not only broke the law, but that they did so willfully and with full knowledge of the consequences of their actions. Your job is first step in administering those consequences, and the first step in restoring order and integrity to our community. I know that Sam and Kadija are guilty, and by the end of the day, you will know that too. Thank you.

THE PEOPLE VS. SPAM

Jonathan Rand

The Defense presents its case in a most controversial trial—America is suing the junk email industry.

DEFENSE. Your Honor; members of the jury; members of…America. I come before you today to protest a grave injustice. Imagine, if you will, the following scenario: You're walking up and down the aisles of your local supermarket. Suddenly, an intense craving hits you. You decide: What I want right this moment, more than anything in the world, is a thick, juicy steak. So naturally, you do what any decent American would do. You push your shopping cart to the meat section, peruse your options with the friendly man at the counter—whose name is Jim—and decide upon the perfect cut of meat. Sound normal so far? It sure does to me. But no, just as Jim bestows you with the juiciest slab of steak money can buy, just as you are mere seconds from placing it in your cart, a hand appears out of nowhere. This hand wrenches the steak from your grasp—the steak you so desire; the steak you deserve after toiling fifty, sixty, one hundred hours every week for your country; that steak, dripping with the blood of the brave soldiers who fought for our independence some 200 years ago—that very hand removes the steak from your possession, throws it to the floor, kicks it, then looks up and spits in your eye.

Ladies and gentlemen of the jury… This story I present to you is no metaphor. It is an allegory. The steak of which I speak represents the products you desire every day. The man at the meat counter, Jim, represents all honest, hard-working Americans who wish to give you the products you so deserve, be it at a supermarket, or in the inbox of your personal computer. Lastly, the hand which impinged upon your very freedom in the meat section? That hand sits in this courtroom today. That hand is trying to take away the American people's right to receive legitimate email correspondence from respectable vendors across this great land—vendors who wish nothing more than to give you the products you deserve. Products which make us better people, better citizens, and better members...of the human race.

Ladies and gentlemen of the jury, you may be thinking to yourself: How could such an atrocity happen in this land of the free? Surely a civilized nation such as America couldn't possibly stoop so low as to rip away our most basic human rights. You might expect such acts of injustice in developing countries like Zimbabwe or Canada. But the United States of America? Within these majestic purple mountains? Above these plains of fruit? I would hope not. I would certainly hope not. America...America...these plaintiffs shed their DISgrace on thee.

Thank you.

THE SUBWAY

John Augustine

A depressed yet self-assured person dressed in crummy clothes and with a red rubber nose—announces to the subway passengers how funny he/she is. Sincere, rather corny, and not all that funny, he is really, after all—just asking for money.

CLOWN. Ladies and germs. I am a clown. Bet you could not guess. I am not collecting for the homeless, I am just a clown. I have always been a clown. I started out in high school as the class clown…and just went on from there. I briefly attended clown college in Florida. But they only teach you how to be a clown in the circus. I have what you might call a really good sense of humor. I don't know where it comes from. But like sometimes, I'll just be standing somewhere and somebody will say something, and then I'll say something, and it will be very funny. Usually people will laugh and wonder where I get my sense of humor. Not from Clown College I can tell you that right now. Humor is a God-given talent they used to say to me…

Or sometimes I'm on the subway, and I'll start to laugh and people will look at me like I'm crazy and I'll say: Hey! I'm not crazy! I was just thinking something really funny. You see? I can crack myself up. Or sometimes people say to me: Hey! Don't you have any normal clothes? And I say. Hey! What's "normal" anyway? I have a "sister" who's a "lesbian." Besides, these are the only clothes I have…well, not just this outfit, but I mean that I only have clown-esque clothing. Or clothing in the clown genre.

Say, for instance, I want to buy a pair of suspenders. I don't buy a solid color. I go for a rainbow design or some design having to do with clowns. I also like for formal dressing, those black stretch pants with stirrups for your feet.

I enjoy performing mime! You may wish I would perform mime now. Or at least be quiet. *(Louder:)* But I think too many clowns are quiet these days. And besides, I am not prepared to do mime today. Well, ok. But just this one thing. It's called, "The Box." You pretend you are in a box and find all the invisible walls around you. That's fun. I'll do it now. (... ... ...)

Thank you. Oh! And I'm homeless. I'm a Vietnam vet. I'm a real estate broker, and this is my imitation of a smoke alarm. EEEEEEEEEEEE. EEEEEEEEEE. This is not mime. EEEEEEEEEE. Money does make me stop. EEEEEEEE Though I am not asking for money. EEEE EEEEEE Money makes me stop. Money makes me stop. EEEEE Thank you. Thank you.

TALES FROM THE ARABIAN MICE

Will Averill

Rock, a perennial bit player, believes there are small parts for actors. He gripes to the audience.

ROCK. Hi. I don't know if you remember me or not, but I was the kid who played the Crocodile last year in Peter Pan? Do you remember? Probably not. It was a little part, and although I've trained for years for a life in the theatre, three years running here at the [name of venue], they have neglected to use me to my fullest potential…again. You know what I am this year? I'm. a. rock. Not the professional wrestler and famous actor in such cinematic classics as 'The Scorpion King', no, I'm just a routine lousy geological formation which our protagonist (that's a big word for hero that I learned in my three years of professional theatre training, all of which did me NO good when it came to casting), finds himself collapsing against in his time of trouble. Can't wait for school to start again—'We went to Disneyworld this summer, oh, wow, we went to Europe. Hey, what'd you do this summer (kid's name). Who, me? Oh. I stayed at home AND PLAYED A LOUSY 'ROCK!' Not that I'm bitter. Cause it's—

(Uber-sarcastic:)

"—it's great training."

(PIPSQUEAK coughs.)

Oh. Excuse me. Gotta go LIE ON THE FLOOR AND DO NOTHING now for a while.

(ROCK returns to his position.)

THANK YOU FOR FLUSHING MY HEAD IN THE TOILET, AND OTHER RARELY USED EXPRESSIONS

Jonathan Dorf

A student finds an injured bird by the birdbath in the backyard, but just when the student seems poised to play Dr. Doolittle, the story takes a disturbing turn.

BLUEBIRD STUDENT. There's a birdbath in my yard. In the back. We get robins, sparrows, pigeons. A lot of pigeons. Sometimes there's a cardinal. And squirrels. Yeah, I know they're not birds, but maybe the squirrels think they are. I mean there's flying squirrels—right? I've never seen one, but flying squirrels exist. Right?

(Beat.)

I like watching the birds. The real birds. The way they all kinda twitch their heads forward,

(Demonstrates a pecking motion.)

It's like they're talking to each other. Saying how's your day and how's the weather and would you like worms with that order? Sometimes when I'm bored, I make up what they'd say. Like this one pigeon, he's complaining about his taxes to a sparrow, and the sparrow's like, "dude, maybe if you spent more time working and less time looking for handouts in the park..."

(Beat.)

I'm supposed to put water in the birdbath once a week. Today's my day. And the birds are there talking about the weather and their kids and there's a duck talking about how his cousin bought the farm and got served up in orange sauce last week. And the other

---

Actor's Choice: Monologues for Teens (Male or Female)

birds are saying how sad that is and how sorry they are, only this one bird's not talking. He's not even in the bath. He's wet, like he was there, but he's not in there. He's on the ground under the bath, and he's trying to hop up, only he can't. There's something wrong with his left wing. He can't flap it like the right one. And he's spinning around in a circle, like he's break dancing—only he's not.

(*Beat.* ACHILLES *enters silently and watches.*)

I go over to the bath, and they all scatter when I get close. Except for the break dancing bird. It's a bluebird—I don't remember when I've ever seen a bluebird in our backyard, and now there's one spinning like a merry-go-round under the birdbath. He's beautiful. He's flapping his right wing like crazy, but the poor little guy can't go anywhere. And he's going nuts when I pick him up in my hands. I hold him real tight so he doesn't scratch me, and I've got my thumb and finger around his neck to keep him from biting. "Don't worry, little bird. I've got you." And I hold him.

(*Beat.*)

The phone rings in the house. I'm the only one home, but I don't move. I've got this beautiful, living thing in my hands, and that's more important than—

(*Beat.*)

The longer I hold him, the less he fights. He knows he's safe. I'm like the Dr. Doolittle of my backyard.

(*Beat.*)

And then I start to squeeze my finger and thumb together. Around his neck. Around *its* neck. Tighter and tighter. The bluebird starts going crazy. I know it can't breathe, and I don't stop. I keep going—because I can. I keep going until it's— It feels good. It feels good, because for once in my life, I'm not the bird.